D1031646

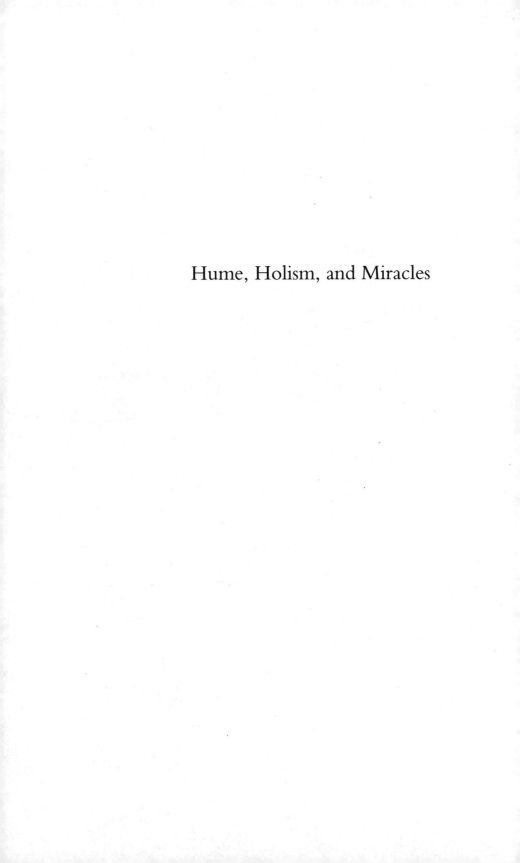

Hume, Holism, and Miracles

A volume in the series

Cornell Studies in the Philosophy of Religion

EDITED BY WILLIAM P. ALSTON

A full list of titles in the series appears at the end of the book.

David Johnson

HUME, HOLISM, AND MIRACLES

Cornell University Press, Ithaca and London

First published 1999 by Cornell University Press

Printed in the United States of America

Library of Congress Cataloging-in-Publication Data

Johnson, David, b.1952
Hume, holism, and miracles / David Johnson.
p.   cm. — (Cornell studies in the philosophy of religion)
Includes bibliographical references and index.
ISBN 0-8014-3663-x (alk. paper)
1. Hume, David, 1711–1776—Views on miracles.   2. Miracles—History of doctrines—
18th century.   I. Title.   II. Series.
B1499.M5J64   1999
212—dc21   99-37179

Cloth printing   10   9   8   7   6   5   4   3   2   1

To my mother, June, and my brother, Edward

Eloquence, when at its highest pitch, leaves little room for reason or reflection; but addressing itself entirely to the fancy or the affections, captivates the willing hearers, and subdues their understanding.

—David Hume, "Of Miracles"

Contents

Acknowledgments

The brief first chapter of this book will indicate to the reader the nature of the work. Here I will simply express my gratitude, for very helpful comments, to the editor of the series, William Alston, to Robert Audi, to my brother Edward Johnson (who also typed the manuscript), to my colleagues Rabbi Shalom Carmy and David Shatz, and to my students Joshua Abraham, Jonathan Douek, and Meir Soloveichik. I am also very grateful to Dean Norman Adler and Yeshiva University for providing me with resources, mundane and divine.

I should note that the second section of the seventh chapter discusses a few modest technicalities, and could be skipped on a first reading of the book.

D. A. J.

the first day of Rosh Hashanah, 1998

Hume, Holism, and Miracles

Promissory Note

Toward the end of Hume's essay "Of Miracles," he states his final conclusion that "no human testimony can have such force as to prove a miracle, and make it a just foundation for any such system of religion." [1] The
sort of "system of religion" at issue is that of "popular religions." What
does Hume mean by "popular religions"? I think he means simply any religion—any theological worldview—which is evidentially based chiefly
or solely on the alleged occurrence of miracles: such religions as the Christianity of most Christians who have lived and (as I would say, though this
is rather more controversial) the Judaism of most Jews who have lived. So
I take Hume's final conclusion to be that no human testimony can have
such force as to prove a miracle and make it a just foundation (a proper
main or solitary evidential basis) for any system of religion that is evidentially based chiefly or solely on the alleged occurrence of miracles. Simpli-
fying this in an uncontroversial way, we may say that the conclusion is that
no human testimony can have such force as to prove a miracle and make it
a just *foundation for a system of religion*. Hume himself restates his conclusion
in the following paragraph as: "a miracle can never be proved, so as to be

---

[1] David Hume, *An Enquiry concerning Human Understanding*, section 10 (henceforth: "Of
Miracles"), in *Enquiries concerning Human Understanding and concerning the Principles of Morals*,
by David Hume, ed. L. A. Selby-Bigge, 2d ed. (Oxford: Clarendon Press, 1902), 127. (P. H.
Nidditch has edited a third edition of the Selby-Bigge volume [1975], but [except in one
very trivial instance] his textual changes do not affect any of the passages with which we are
concerned.) The first edition of *Philosophical Essays concerning Human Understanding* (as the
work was originally called) was published in 1748.

the foundation of a system of religion," it being understood that the only kind of proof available is "proof from human testimony."

How is Hume supposed to be establishing this conclusion? His essay is divided into two parts. The burden of the first part is that of, as Richard Swinburne has put it, "showing on philosophical grounds that the evidence against the occurrence of any purported miracle is normally likely to be extremely strong and to outweigh by far the evidence in favor of the occurrence."[2] (The word 'normally' is inserted by Swinburne because, as we will see later, Hume allows that in certain imaginary cases of exotically strong testimonial evidence in favor of a miracle, we ought to believe that the miracle has occurred.) The burden of the second part of Hume's essay is that of showing, mostly on supposed historical and psychohistorical grounds, that the evidence in favor of such miracles as have actually been alleged to occur is extremely weak indeed, and that when such a purported miracle is, as Hume says, "ascribed to any new system of religion," then "this very circumstance would be a full proof of a cheat, and sufficient, with all men of sense, not only to make them reject the fact, but even reject it without farther examination."[3] This conclusion has *something* to do with, at least, the alleged fact that "men, in all ages, have been . . . much imposed on by ridiculous stories of that kind," and the alleged fact that "violations of truth are more common in the testimony concerning religious miracles, than in that concerning any other matter of fact."[4]

In this book, I focus on the argument of the first part of Hume's essay, on the "main argument," as J. L. Mackie calls it,[5] on the "philosophical grounds" of which Swinburne speaks. I will explain why I think that these philosophical grounds are entirely specious. It is indeed a view strangely prevailing amongst philosophers that Hume has given in the first part of his essay, or one can reconstruct from Hume's remarks, some at least prima facie good argument for the conclusion that, where m is an alleged miracle, allegedly witnessed, and where L is an apparent law of nature, which law m's occurrence would violate, and where (thus) L is exceedingly well supported (and m's occurrence is exceedingly improbable) relative to a body of inductive evidence, then—at the very least—the testimony of one hu-

---

[2] Introduction to *Miracles*, ed. Richard Swinburne (New York: Macmillan, 1989), 11.
[3] Hume, "Of Miracles," 128, 129.
[4] Ibid., 128–129, 129.
[5] J. L. Mackie, *The Miracle of Theism: Arguments for and against the Existence of God* (Oxford: Clarendon Press, 1982), 16.

man witness who claims to have observed m's occurrence can never rightly convince us that m has occurred; the testimony of one such supposed witness to m's occurrence will always be "outweighed" by the inductive evidence which so strongly supports L. Even Swinburne (who in the end is not persuaded by it) says that "Hume's argument is a powerful one."[6] Mackie, reconstructing Hume's argument in a way we will look at later, says that Hume has found "a very powerful reply to any claim that a miracle has been performed."[7] Antony Flew speaks of Hume's "devastating objection."[8] And, as often as such remarks are made in print, doubtless they are made even more often in the lecture room, or in (necessarily, as we will see) casual conversation. (To my utter astonishment, I have heard it reported of a certain eminent *logician*, that because of reading Hume's essay, he could never again take seriously the claim that Jesus had risen from the dead.)

I trust that I am saying nothing controversial if I add that the perception that there is some such strong Humean argument (either Hume's own, or one like it)—at least for the weaker than usual version of the Humean conclusion which I have given in the preceding paragraph—has taken a deep hold on the Western intellect. (Of course, if no Humean argument establishes that weaker conclusion, then no Humean argument establishes the customary stronger version, not solely about the limitations of the force of *one* human being's testimony.) When the nineteenth-century French biblical scholar Ernest Renan, because no miracle has ever been observed under rigorous "conditions scientifiques," proposes that "we banish miracles from history" and "that a report of the supernatural cannot be accepted as such, that it always implies credulity or imposture";[9] or when the nineteenth-century German biblical scholar David Strauss informs us (straightway, as Saint Mark might say) that "in the person and the work of Jesus there is nothing supernatural";[10] or when the contemporary historian

---

[6] Swinburne, 12.

[7] Mackie, 26.

[8] Antony Flew, Introduction to *An Enquiry concerning Human Understanding*, by David Hume (La Salle, Ill.: Open Court, 1988), xviii.

[9] My translation of: "nous bannissons le miracle de l'histoire"; "qu'un récit surnaturel ne peut être admis comme tel, qu'il implique toujours crédulité ou imposture." Ernest Renan, *Vie de Jésus*, 13th ed. (Paris: Calmann-Lévy, 1876), xcv–xcvi, xcviii.

[10] My translation of: "in der Person und dem Werke Jesu nichts Uebernatürliches . . . ist." *Das Leben Jesu für das deutsche Volk bearbeitet von David Friedrich Strauss* (Stuttgart: Alfred Kröner, 1905), xxiv. This work was first published at Leipzig by F. A. Brockhaus in 1864.

Michael Grant, in considering whether a certain supposed appearance of
the resurrected Jesus to Saint Peter was "a delusion," says that "so, to the
rational mind, it has to be"[11]—what can such claims by non-philosophers
possibly be based on except some argument of the Humean kind?[12]

But the view that there is in Hume's essay, or in what can be reconstructed from it, any argument or reply or objection that is even super-
ficially good, much less, powerful or devastating, is simply a philosophical
myth. The mostly willing hearers who have been swayed by Hume on
this matter have been held captive by nothing other than Hume's great
eloquence.

---

[11] Michael Grant, *Saint Peter: A Biography* (New York: Scribner, 1994), 100.
[12] Strauss, at least, seems to have been directly influenced by Hume. See the work cited,
188–191.

[2]

'Miracle', 'Violation', 'Law of Nature'

Before we proceed to the main issue, we must address a well-known problem concerning Hume's definition of 'miracle'. Hume gives two definitions:

> A miracle is a violation of the laws of nature;[1] A miracle may be accurately defined, *a transgression of a law of nature by a particular volition of the Deity, or by the interposition of some invisible agent.*[2]

For now, let us set aside the question of the relation of a miracle to a god, and focus on the notion of a miracle as a "violation" (or "transgression") of a "law" (or of the laws) of nature. The prima facie difficulty here has been well explained by Mackie:

> A miracle is, by definition, a violation of a law of nature, and a law of nature is, by definition, a regularity—or the statement of a regularity—about what happens, about the way the world works; consequently, if some event actually occurs, no regularity which its occurrence infringes (or, no regularity-statement which it falsifies) can really be a law of nature; so this event, however unusual or surprising, cannot after all be a miracle. The two definitions together entail that whatever happens is not a miracle, that is, that

---

[1] Hume, "Of Miracles," 114. (It is perhaps not entirely obvious that this is intended as a *definition*. But it is traditionally regarded as such, and here I shall follow tradition.)

[2] Ibid., 115 n. 1.

miracles never happen. This, be it noted, is not Hume's argument. If it were correct, it would make Hume's argument unnecessary. Before we discuss Hume's case, then, we should consider whether there is a coherent concept of a miracle which would not thus rule out the occurrence of miracles *a priori*.[3]

Hume never tells us what a law of nature is. But if we adopt a view of laws of nature which is presumably very congenial to Hume's general philosophy, that a law of nature is (or expresses) *at least* an exceptionless regularity (or, at least, is, or corresponds to, a true universal generalization), then, since a "violation" or "transgression" of such a law would presumably be at least an *exception* to it, and since we know a priori that there are no exceptions to exceptionless regularities, we know a priori that there are no miracles, if we know a priori that a miracle is a violation of the laws of nature. As Mackie notes, this clearly will not do. It is abundantly clear that Hume means to be using 'miracle' in *some* sense such that we neither know a priori that there are no miracles, nor even know a priori that there are no miracles rightly established by human testimony. Hume writes:

> I beg the limitations here made may be remarked, when I say, that a miracle can never be proved, so as to be the foundation of a system of religion. For I own, that otherwise, there may possibly be miracles, or violations of the usual course of nature, of such a kind as to admit of proof from human testimony; though, perhaps, it will be impossible to find any such in all the records of history. Thus, suppose, all authors, in all languages, agree, that, from the first of January 1600, there was a total darkness over the whole earth for eight days: suppose that the tradition of this extraordinary event is still strong and lively among the people: that all travellers, who return from foreign countries, bring us accounts of the same tradition, without the least variation or contradiction: it is evident, that our present philosophers, instead of doubting the fact, ought to receive it as certain, and ought to search for the causes whence it might be derived. The decay, corruption, and dissolution of nature, is an event rendered probable by so many analogies, that any phenomenon, which seems to have a tendency towards that catastrophe, comes within the reach of human testimony, if that testimony be very extensive and uniform.[4]

[3] Mackie, 19.
[4] Hume, "Of Miracles," 127–128.

If we begin, naturally enough, with the notion that a miracle is "a violation of the laws of nature," then, to stave off an illusory a priori proof that there are no miracles, we must tinker either with the definition of 'miracle' itself, or with the definition of 'violation', or with the definition of 'laws of nature'. Mackie opts for the third of these strategies. He introduces the notion of "basic laws of working." The reader should consult Mackie's own extended discussion of this matter in the eighth and ninth chapters of *The Cement of the Universe*,[5] but perhaps a crude analogy will help. We might say that it is a "law of working" for a certain electronic device that, say, all red-button pushings are radio-playings. We might say that this is a sort of "law" for the mechanism, even though it is false—because I unplug the machine, or smash it, so that some red-button pushings are not radio-playings. Mackie's idea is that there are *basic* "laws of working" for the world, which can be violated (have exceptions) and still be laws, in that they "describe the ways in which the world . . . works when left to itself, when not interfered with." He says:

> If miracles are to serve their traditional function of giving spectacular support to religious claims . . . the concept must not be so weakened that anything at all unusual or remarkable counts as a miracle. We must keep in the definition the notion of a violation of natural law. But then, if it is to be even possible that a miracle should occur, we must modify the definition given above of a law of nature. What we want to do is to contrast the order of nature with a possible divine or supernatural intervention. The laws of nature, we must say, describe the ways in which the world . . . works when left to itself, when not interfered with. A miracle occurs when the world is not left to itself, when something distinct from the natural order as a whole intrudes into it. . . . For our present purpose . . . it is not essential that we should . . . be approaching an understanding of how the world works; it is enough that we have the concept of such basic laws of working, that we know in principle what it would be to discover them. Once we have this concept, we have moved beyond the definition of laws of nature merely as (statements of) what always happens. We can see how, using this concept and using the assumption that there are some such basic laws of working to be found, we can hope to determine what the actual laws of working are by reference to a restricted range of experiments and observations. This opens up the pos-

---

[5] J. L. Mackie, *The Cement of the Universe: A Study of Causation* (Oxford: Oxford University Press, 1974).

sibility that we might determine that something *is* a basic law of working of natural objects, and yet also, independently, find that it was occasionally violated. An occasional violation does not in itself necessarily overthrow the independently established conclusion that this *is* a law of working.[6]

Swinburne suggests that we tinker with *both* the notion of a law of nature and the notion of a violation.[7] Roughly, the idea seems to be that a law of nature is a (universal or statistical, probabilistic or nonprobabilistic) generalization which is *true or almost true* and which is (never?) in genuine competition with any alternative (incompatible?) law-candidate. (This touches on issues in the general theory of confirmation—"projectibility," "simplicity," etc.—which Swinburne discusses but which I will not go into here. I have discussed some of them elsewhere.)[8] Swinburne (following Ninian Smart) suggests that a *violation* of a law of nature is "a nonrepeatable counter-instance" to it: "an exception that would not be repeated under similar circumstances."[9] (So a violation of a law of nature is still at least an *exception* to it, which is why Swinburne must tinker as well with the notion of a law of nature.)

I find much of what Swinburne says here deeply mysterious, but since in any event I prefer, for present purposes, a *simpler* way of tinkering—introducing an explicitly time-indexed and *epistemic* notion of what a miracle is—I will not further discuss what Swinburne and Mackie suggest. I doubt that the merits of my criticisms of Hume in any way hinge on this choice.

I think, also, that the substance of what I have to say about Hume does not in any essential way turn on issues having to do with whether the laws of nature are universal or statistical, probabilistic or nonprobabilistic (interesting though such issues are vis-à-vis the notion of a miracle).[10] Solely for the sake of simplicity, then, in trying to expound Hume's (or a Hum-

---

[6] Mackie, *Miracle of Theism*, 19–21.

[7] Richard Swinburne, *The Concept of Miracle* (London: Macmillan, 1970), chap. 3.

[8] David Johnson, "Induction and Modality," *Philosophical Review* 100:3 (July 1991): 399–430.

[9] Swinburne, ed., *Miracles*, 9. The work by Ninian Smart which Swinburne follows is *Philosophers and Religious Truth* (London: SCM Press, 1964), chap. 2, "Miracles and David Hume."

[10] See Peter van Inwagen's beautiful chapter, "The Place of Chance in a World Sustained by God," in *Divine and Human Action: Essays in the Metaphysics of Theism*, ed. Thomas V. Morris (Ithaca: Cornell University Press, 1988), 211–235.

ean) argument here and explain what is fundamentally wrong with it, I will assume, as in effect I suppose that Hume did, that the *laws* of nature, whatever else they may be, are (or are expressed by, or correspond to, or imply, contingent) universal and nonprobabilistic generalizations which, furthermore, are *true*. (Surely, in making these assumptions, I am not in any way weakening Hume's case.) I will say, then, that for any person *x*, for any time *t*, for any possible event *m*, *m* is a *miracle* for *x* at *t* if and only if *m* actually occurs at some time and *m* is a violation of (an exception to) something which is for *x* at *t* exceedingly well established, relative to a body of inductive evidence, as being a law of nature. (This, of course, does not imply that a miracle for *x* at *t* must *occur at t.*) More pithily, I will say that *a miracle is a violation of an apparent law of nature*, where the indexing to person and time, and the epistemic aspect above, is built into the word 'apparent'.[11]

In the above definition, let the *inductive evidence* be as proper as we philosophers like. Let it be a collection of *A*s that are *B*s, but not just any such collection—rather, one that is large, wide-ranging, etc. And let us grant, with Antony Flew, that the inductive evidence (or some of it) must be, as Flew puts it, not "merely passive *experience*," but *sought out* through "active tests of reliability," so that the apparent law is "thoroughly tested for reliability, whether directly on its own account separately, or indirectly via the testing of some wider structure of theory from which it follows as a consequence."[12] (Granting Flew's requirement does not, as we will see, strengthen Hume's case.) And let us stipulate that, of course, no generalization can be, for anyone at any time, exceedingly well established, relative to such a body of inductive evidence, as being a law of nature, if that person at that time knows that there are *generally known* (or *uncontroversially known*) cases of *A*s that are not *B*s.

We seek, then, Hume's (or a Humean) argument for at least the weaker

---

[11] It is possible, though I make no claim that it is actually so, that something like this is what Hume really meant by 'miracle'. Consider Hume's interesting choice of words when he says: "Where such reports, therefore, fly about, the solution of the phenomenon is obvious; and we judge in conformity to regular experience and observation, when we account for it by the known and natural principles of credulity and delusion. And shall we, rather than have a recourse to so natural a solution, allow of a miraculous violation of the most established laws of nature?" ("Of Miracles," 126).

[12] Antony Flew, *Hume's Philosophy of Belief: A Study of His First* Inquiry (London: Routledge and Kegan Paul, 1961), 206.

than usual version of Hume's conclusion (of the first part of his essay) mentioned in the preceding chapter, which we now state in the following way:

(H) Where m is a possible event, allegedly actual and allegedly witnessed, and where L is (for us, now) an apparent law, which any actual occurrence of m would have violated, and where (thus) L is (for us, now) exceedingly well established, relative to a body of inductive evidence, as being a law of nature, then, at the very least, the testimony of *one* human witness (not identical to any of us) who claims to have observed m's occurrence can never rightly convince us that m has occurred—the testimony of *one* such supposed witness to m's occurrence will always be "outweighed" by the inductive evidence which so strongly supports L.

[3]

Hume's Own Argument

I have a certain fear, that some readers upon reading the present chapter may say, "Oh, that again!" and fail to read the rest of this book, thus missing something about which they would most certainly not make the same remark. So let me make it clear: the difficulty which I am about to describe in Hume's own argument has nothing to do with my own criticisms of the sort of *Humean* argument at issue. We will come to these criticisms when we examine various reconstructions of Hume's argument. But the present difficulty must be explained both for its own sake and so that the reader will appreciate why the argument must be *reconstructed*.

In setting out Hume's argument, more or less as he himself presents it — as involving "proof against proof, of which the strongest must prevail"[1] — we must begin by considering what Hume means by 'proof'. In a footnote at the beginning of the sixth section ("Of Probability") of the *Enquiry*, Hume says that:

> Mr. Locke divides all arguments into demonstrative and probable. In this view, we must say, that it is only probable all men must die, or that the sun will rise to-morrow. But to conform our language more to common use, we ought to divide arguments into *demonstrations*, *proofs*, and *probabilities*. By proofs meaning such arguments from experience as leave no room for doubt or opposition.[2]

---

[1] Hume, "Of Miracles", 114.
[2] Hume, *An Enquiry concerning Human Understanding* (Selby-Bigge edition), 56 n. 1.

It is not, I think, altogether obvious that Hume intends "such arguments from experience as leave no room for doubt or opposition" to be the very *definition* of 'proof'. (As is well known to philosophers, that one uses 'meaning' or its cognates does not necessarily mean that one is giving a suggested *meaning* for a term or phrase.) If Hume does so intend, there is then the interesting question of whether the phrase "leave no room for doubt or opposition" is to be taken in a merely psychological or in a *normative* sense. But such questions need not detain us. In the essay "Of Miracles," Hume says:

> A wise man . . . proportions his belief to the evidence. In such conclusions as are founded on an infallible experience, he expects the event with the last degree of assurance, and regards his past experience as a full *proof* of the future existence of that event. In other cases, he proceeds with more caution: He weighs the opposite experiments: He considers which side is supported by the greater number of experiments: to that side he inclines, with doubt and hesitation; and when at last he fixes his judgement, the evidence exceeds not what we properly call *probability*. All probability, then, supposes an opposition of experiments and observations.[3]

The above passages make it clear, I think, that for present purposes we need not worry very much about whether it is part of the very *notion* of a proof that it be such as to "leave no room for doubt or opposition," or similarly whether it is part of its very notion that it gives "the last degree of assurance," and so (happily) we need not dwell on the meaning or legitimate application here of such phrases. (Hume *might* simply have held that such phrases indicate a salient characteristic *of* proofs.) For present purposes, all we need is the abundantly clear fact that Hume holds that every *nonstatistical inductive inference* we make—every inference we make of the form *all hitherto observed* (examined, relevantly tested, etc.) A*s are B*s, hence all A*s are B*s, where *we know that the inductive premiss is true*—is a "proof," and vice versa. In short, the *proofs* are (in fact, whether by definition or not) all and only the given *nonstatistical inductions with known premisses*. I say that this is abundantly clear. In the first passage from Hume quoted above, the division of arguments into demonstrations, proofs, and probabilities is surely intended to be exhaustive and exclusive. Now, consider any given nonstatistical induction with known premiss. It is an argument. But it is obviously

---

3 Hume, "Of Miracles," 110–111.

not a demonstration. Nor can it be a probability, since "All probability . . . supposes an opposition of experiments and observations." So it must be a *proof.* Now consider any proof. Where we have a proof we must have a given induction with known premiss, since a proof is an argument "from experience." But it cannot be a statistical induction with known premiss, since then it would be a *probability.* "In other cases . . . the evidence exceeds not what we properly call *probability.*" So it must be a nonstatistical induction with known premiss. Proofs are (in fact, whether by definition or not) all and only those given "arguments from experience" which are "founded on an *infallible* experience" (my emphasis).

If any doubt remains on the point, consider Hume's further remark: "as the evidence, derived from witnesses and human testimony, is founded on past experience, so it varies with the experience, and is regarded either as a *proof* or a *probability,* according as the conjunction between any particular kind of report and any kind of object has been found to be constant or variable."[4] Note the words "according as." It would be very odd if what Hume asserts about *this* kind of argument "founded on past experience" did not reflect a *general* fact about arguments "from experience": where and only where "the conjunction" of *A* and *B* "has been found to be" *constant,* we have a *proof,* and where and only where it has been found to be *variable,* we have a *probability.*

Despite the apparent clarity of the above, the point has been denied. Since the claim that Hume holds that *every proof is a nonstatistical induction with known premiss* is crucial to the forthcoming charge that he, in a superficial sense, begs the question, let us stop for a minute and consider what reason has been given for denying the above. (I beg the reader's indulgence here. Although the present matter is philosophically irrelevant to the larger issue about miracles, it is exegetically and historically important, since on it turns entirely the merit of that *often made charge* that Hume himself begs the question.) David Owen has written:

> One bit of evidence . . . is mentioned by I. Hacking in another context ("Hume's Species of Probability," *Philosophical Studies* 33 (1978) pp. 21–37). Hacking points out (pp. 27–28) that while Hume allows, in theory, a species of probability connected with exceptionless uniformities, he further claims that in fact "no one who is arrived at the age of maturity can any longer be acquainted with it" *(Treatise of Human Nature,* Book I Part III Sec-

[4] Ibid., 112.

tion XII). So unless in maturity we also lose our acquaintance with proofs, proofs cannot be based on exceptionless experience.[5]

It seems to me that the above is based on a misreading of what Hume says in the *Treatise*. Here is the relevant passage:

> The probabilities of causes are of several kinds; but are all deriv'd from the same origin, *viz. the association of ideas to a present impression*. As the habit, which produces the association, arises from the frequent conjunction of objects, it must arrive at its perfection by degrees, and must acquire new force from each instance, that falls under our observation. The first instance has little or no force: The second makes some addition to it: The third becomes still more sensible; and 'tis by these slow steps, that our judgment arrives at a full assurance. But before it attains this pitch of perfection, it passes thro' several inferior degrees, and in all of them is only to be esteem'd a presumption or probability. The gradation, therefore, from probabilities to proofs is in many cases insensible; and the difference betwixt these kinds of evidence is more easily perceiv'd in the remote degrees, than in the near and contiguous.
>
> 'Tis worthy of remark on this occasion, that tho' the species of probability here explain'd be the first in order, and naturally takes place before any entire proof can exist, yet no one, who is arriv'd at the age of maturity, can any longer be acquainted with it. 'Tis true, nothing is more common than for people of the most advanc'd knowledge to have attain'd only an imperfect experience of many particular events; which naturally produces only an imperfect habit and transition: But then we must consider, that the mind, having form'd another observation concerning the connexion of causes and effects, gives new force to its reasoning from that observation; and by means of it can build an argument on one single experiment, when duly prepar'd and examin'd. What we have found once to follow from any object, we conclude will for ever follow from it; and if this maxim be not always built upon as certain, 'tis not for want of a sufficient number of experiments, but because we frequently meet with instances to the contrary; which leads us to the second species of probability, where there is a *contrariety* in our experience and observation.[6]

---

[5] David Owen, "Hume *versus* Price on Miracles and Prior Probabilities: Testimony and the Bayesian Calculation," *Philosophical Quarterly* 37 (1987): 190 n. 6.

[6] David Hume, *A Treatise of Human Nature*, edited by L. A. Selby-Bigge (Oxford: Clarendon Press, 1888), 130–131. The *Treatise* was first published in 1739–40.

The "species of probability" which "no one, who is arriv'd at the age of maturity, can any longer be acquainted with" is that of "the probability of causes" *construed as* a kind of probability which moves "from probabilities to proofs" (which arrives at "its perfection") "by degrees" and "by these slow steps." Hume is not in any obvious way saying that in our maturity we lose our acquaintance with probabilities which are, as Owen says, "based on exceptionless experience." Perhaps the meaning of the obscure second paragraph is that a proof is where "the mind, having form'd another observation concerning the connexion of causes and effects"—having acquired, I take it, the general notion of causation—thereafter even from a *single case* of conjoined objects makes (in the absence of observed contrariety) a *perfect* "habit and transition" from this sort of cause to this sort of effect; the mind concludes that these objects will always come conjoined in the even once observed way. But then *how* is the transition not "based on exceptionless experience"? For it must still be the case that the conjunction has *always* been observed by the mind, else there were contrariety. Nor do I see any compelling evidence *here* (since it is not at all clear what Hume means when he says that "nothing is more common than for people of the most advanc'd knowledge to have attain'd only an imperfect experience of many particular events") that Hume is making a distinction between exceptionless personal experience and exceptionless experience of some more global human kind, though *perhaps* the issue of human testimony is arising here in a veiled form. (Such a distinction is indeed of the first importance, and arises quite explicitly, albeit ambiguously, in the essay "Of Miracles." We will be much exercised by it later.)

But, in any event, whatever the author of the *Treatise* may have meant, it cannot possibly be the case that the author of the *Enquiry* supposed that in our maturity we lose our acquaintance with nonstatistical inductions with known premises; for the latter is well acquainted with such arguments. In the sixth section of the *Enquiry* ("Of Probability"), which is, of course, the analogue of, in part, the section of the *Treatise* ("Of the probability of causes") from which we have quoted above, Hume says:

> There are some causes, which are entirely uniform and constant in producing a particular effect; and no instance has ever yet been found of any failure or irregularity in their operation. Fire has always burned, and water suffocated every human creature: The production of motion by impulse and gravity is an universal law, which has hitherto admitted of no exception. . . .

> Being determined by custom to transfer the past to the future, in all our in-
> ferences; where the past has been entirely regular and uniform, we expect
> the event with the greatest assurance, and leave no room for any contrary
> supposition.[7]

Note the familiar-sounding words, "we expect the event with the greatest
assurance, and leave no room for any contrary supposition." I take these
words (whether their sense is merely psychological, or normative) to express what Hume holds is a salient characteristic *of* proofs. The proofs
themselves I take to be those inferences from experience "where the past
has been entirely regular and uniform." (And it is indeed *evident* that "such
arguments from experience as leave no room for doubt or opposition," or
some like phrase, cannot itself really be Hume's *definition* of 'proof'. For, if
it were, its sense must be either merely psychological, or normative. In the
first case, Hume's later *premiss* that there is always a "proof" against a miracle would be obviously false. Hume himself gives counterexamples to
such a claim in his discussion of the miracles "upon the tomb of Abbé
Paris."[8] In the second case, the "premiss" would be *so obviously* question-
begging as to be simply silly. Such a premiss, where 'proof' is *defined* by the
above phrase read in a normative sense, is essentially Hume's *conclusion*.)

We return, then, to Hume's own argument. The argument, it seems to
me, is presented, somewhat implicitly, in three passages from the first part
of Hume's essay:

> in order to encrease the probability against the testimony of witnesses, let us
> suppose, that the fact, which they affirm, instead of being only marvellous,
> is really miraculous; and suppose also, that the testimony considered apart
> and in itself, amounts to an entire proof; in that case, there is proof against
> proof, of which the strongest must prevail.[9]

> A miracle is a violation of the laws of nature; and as a firm and unalter-
> able experience has established these laws, the proof against a miracle, from
> the very nature of the fact, is as entire as any argument from experience can
> possibly be imagined.[10]

> And as a uniform experience amounts to a proof, there is here a direct and

---

[7] Hume, *An Enquiry concerning Human Understanding* (Selby-Bigge edition), 57–58.
[8] Ibid., 124.
[9] Ibid., 114.
[10] Ibid.

full *proof*, from the nature of the fact, against the existence of any miracle; nor can such a proof be destroyed, or the miracle rendered credible, but by an opposite proof, which is superior.[11]

In order to simplify the presentation of Hume's argument, so that we may ignore Hume's later caveat about cases of exotically strong human testimony (as in the passage about the eight days of darkness), and so that we may thus ignore what seems to me to be an illusory or at least not very important difficulty for Hume's present argument, I will restrict my consideration to those alleged miracles for which there is the testimony of only *one* human witness, so that we are looking for an argument for the conclusion (H), mentioned in the preceding chapter. (I assume that exotically strong human testimony must be, at least, the testimony of many.) We will see that, even so, there is a certain well-known apparent difficulty in Hume's own argument. If Hume's own argument fails (though on shallow grounds) even when this restriction is made, it would fare no better without it.

I will read, then, the above three passages as indicating the following argument. Whenever a single human witness, of whatever apparent fine character and however seemingly sincere, and so forth, claims to have observed the occurrence of a miracle—a violation of an apparent law of nature or, as Hume later says, of "the most established" laws of nature—we must consider the case for believing that the witness tells the truth, so that the miracle occurred, and the case for believing otherwise. We have *in favor* of the miracle, I suppose, since in this first part of the essay Hume is supposing that the testimony may "amount to" a proof, the conjunction of the following two items, of which only the latter is a *proof* as such:

(i) Some witness of type α says that he observed the miracle occur.
(ii) All hitherto observed (that is, tested for accuracy) witnesses of type α are completely accurate reporters.
  Hence: All witnesses of type α are completely accurate reporters.

The conjunction of (i) with the *conclusion* of (ii) entails the occurrence of the miracle. *Against* the miracle we have a *proof*—Hume is here assuming—of some (apparent) law of nature which the occurrence of the mir-

---

[11] Ibid., 115.

acle would violate. But this latter proof, since it is a *proof*, is "founded on an infallible experience," is based on an inductive premiss which describes "a firm and unalterable experience," etc., and so *this* proof is "as entire as any argument from experience can possibly be imagined." So, at the very least, the proof (ii)—which provides (i) with *all* of (i)'s evidential force—will not be stronger than or "superior" to the proof of the apparent law of nature. Hence the evidence in favor of the miracle is *at the very least not stronger* than the evidence against the miracle. Hence in these circumstances, which must hold "from the very nature of the fact," we cannot *rightly* be convinced that the miracle has occurred.

More details could be added to the above. The general subject of competing nonstatistical inductions could be broached, which would require discussing how large and wide-ranging, how thoroughly sought out, the samples described in the inductive premisses of the above proofs are with respect to each other—none of which, of course, would damage Hume's argument. But we need not go into all of that here, for Hume has already made an apparently serious error.

Hume apparently begs the question. The issue on the table is whether we should believe a witness who claims to have observed a miracle, an *A* that is not a *B*. Hume, I have suggested, assumes that (at least where the miracle is attested to by only one witness) we have against the miracle a proof, so that in particular we have a known inductive premiss, describing "a uniform experience," to the effect that all hitherto observed *A*s are *B*s. But the question of whether we know so general an inductive premiss is essentially the same as the question of whether we know that the *A* observed by the witness was a *B*, or (as the witness claims) not a *B*. Thus, C. S. Lewis famously objects to Hume:

> Now of course we must agree with Hume that if there is absolutely "uniform experience" against miracles, if in other words they have never happened, why then they never have. Unfortunately we know the experience against them to be uniform only if we know that all the reports of them are false. And we can know all the reports to be false only if we know already that miracles have never occurred. In fact, we are arguing in a circle. . . . The question, "Do miracles occur?" and the question, "Is the course of Nature absolutely uniform?" are the same question asked in two different ways. Hume, by sleight of hand, treats them as two different questions. He first answers "Yes," to the question whether Nature is absolutely uniform: and then uses this "Yes" as a ground for answering, "No," to the question, "Do

miracles occur?" The single real question which he set out to answer is never discussed at all. He gets the answer to one form of the question by assuming the answer to another form of the same question.[12]

Hume might, and in at least some moods certainly would, protest that he is not just *assuming* that we have a proof, and hence "a uniform experience," against a given miracle, but that this follows from the very fact that the alleged event is a miracle. "There must . . . be a uniform experience against every miraculous event, otherwise the event would not merit that appellation."[13] But if this is the claim, then, *first*, Hume is saying that it is a necessary truth that every miracle is opposed by a uniform experience ("where [I presume for now] the past has been entirely regular and uniform")—that there *must* be a uniform experience against *every* miraculous event—which is difficult to reconcile with what he says about the imaginary but possible *miracle* of the eight days of darkness. (Note that there is no such difficulty if Hume is merely making the assumption which I have attributed to him above, for that assumption does not imply the preceding supposed necessary truth.) And, *second*, Hume's argument would then depend on a tendentious and, one would rightly say, question-begging assumption about what a miracle must be, so that his argument would then be little better than that illusory a priori *demonstration* that there are no miracles. Just as there is no good reason to define the ordinary word 'miracle' as *an exception to an exceptionless regularity*, so too there is no good reason to define it in effect as *a past event of a kind which has never been observed*. If that is what a miracle is, then of course we should believe no one who claims to have observed a miracle, but what of it? That is not what any *enthusiast* ever meant by 'miracle'. (When Moses claims to have observed his staff become a serpent, or when Saint John claims to have observed a formerly dead man prepare breakfast, no believer would ever have been inclined to insist—lest the event not be miraculous—that the witness add: "And, you know, this is the sort of thing which has never been observed, not even by me on this occasion.") Those who believe that miracles have been observed have neither inclination nor obligation to say that miracles have never been observed. For there are far more plausible proposed definitions

---

[12] C. S. Lewis, *Miracles: A Preliminary Study* (New York: Simon and Schuster, 1996), 134–136. This work (in a slightly different form, not affecting this passage) was first published in 1947.

[13] Hume, "Of Miracles," 115.

of the ordinary word 'miracle', which in no way imply that there is any *contradiction* in the notion of someone's *having observed* a miracle; that in no way imply that there is always a *proof* against a miracle, in Hume's apparent sense of 'proof'.

But perhaps we have misunderstood Hume. Let us look closely at a passage which Flew has called "deservedly notorious":[14]

> Nothing is esteemed a miracle, if it ever happen in the common course of nature. It is no miracle that a man, seemingly in good health, should die on a sudden: because such a kind of death, though more unusual than any other, has yet been frequently observed to happen. But it is a miracle, that a dead man should come to life; because that has never been observed in any age or country. There must, therefore, be a uniform experience against every miraculous event, otherwise the event would not merit that appellation.[15]

This passage is notorious because ever so many authors of Christian apologetic works have claimed that the penultimate sentence obviously begs the question. Let us carefully consider, however, the first sentence above (seldom quoted by Hume's critics). Note that Hume does not say that nothing is esteemed a miracle if it is ever observed. He says that nothing is esteemed a miracle if it ever happens in the common course of nature. (And in the passage about the eight days of darkness, the miracle is a violation "of the usual course of nature.") Now, it is not very clear what Hume means by the common, or usual, course of nature. He might mean, at least, any of the following:

  (a) an absolutely uniform observed course of nature, "where the past has been entirely regular and uniform"—where *all* hitherto observed *A*s are *B*s, *all* hitherto observed *C*s are *D*s, and so on;
  (b) an absolutely uniform observed course of nature *when nature is not interfered with* (à la Mackie) by something outside of nature;
  (c) the commonly or usually observed course of nature—where all *or almost all* hitherto observed *A*s are *B*s, all *or almost all* hitherto observed *C*s are *D*s, and so on.

---

[14] Flew, 204. The passage which Flew calls "deservedly notorious" is the one given below, minus the first and last sentences.
[15] Hume, "Of Miracles," 115.

If Hume means either (b) or (c), then there is a corresponding attenuation in the notion of "a uniform experience," and in the notion of a "proof," and he is absolved of the charge that he obviously begs the question. His argument would then move in the direction of the reconstructions which we will examine.

How would we reconcile such a move with the actual words which Hume uses in distinguishing *proofs* from *probabilities*? We should have to say that "an infallible experience" means an experience infallible vis-à-vis the *common* course of nature—read as (b) or (c); that "a firm and unalterable experience" means one firm and unalterable (that is, without variation or *alteration*) vis-à-vis the *common* course of nature; that saying that the conjunction between *A* and *B* is "constant" means constant vis-à-vis the common course of nature, and so on.

But how, then, would we understand Hume's own *argument*? If there is a "proof against a miracle" only in an attenuated sense of 'proof', how is that "as entire as any argument from experience can possibly be imagined"? We can imagine, and there surely are, arguments from experience which are proofs in the stronger sense. And, where some witness of type α claims to have observed a certain miracle (and there is no other testimony in favor of it), whose occurrence would violate some apparent law that all *A*s are *B*s, might it not turn out that all hitherto observed witnesses of type α are completely accurate reporters (that all witnesses of type α who have been tested for accuracy—and let the sample be as large and wide-ranging and thoroughly sought out as we please—have been found to be completely accurate), whereas against the miracle we now have, perhaps, only an attenuated proof based on a premiss which says only that all or almost all hitherto observed *A*s are *B*s? What then would happen in the conflict of "proof against proof, of which the strongest must prevail"?

It seems, then, that Hume's own argument either obviously begs the question, or becomes obscure, and so we must turn to the reconstructions of "Hume's argument." If anyone claims that one of these reconstructed arguments is what Hume really meant, or "what Hume was up to in the argument about miracles,"[16] I am perfectly happy to agree. For these other arguments most certainly beg the question, in their own and deeper way.

---

[16] Owen, 187.

[4]

Hume's Argument as
Reconstructed by J. L. Mackie

Here is what Mackie says:

any problems there may be about establishing laws of nature are neutral between the parties to the present debate, Hume's followers and those who believe in miracles; for both these parties need the notion of a well-established
law of nature. The miracle advocate needs it in order to be able to say that
the alleged occurrence is a miracle, a violation of natural law by supernatural intervention, no less than Hume needs it for his argument against believing that this event has actually taken place. . . . [T]he defender of a miracle . . . must in effect *concede* to Hume that the antecedent improbability of
this event is as high as it could be, hence that, apart from the testimony, we
have the strongest possible grounds for believing that the alleged event did
not occur. This event must, by the miracle advocate's own admission, be
contrary to a genuine, not merely a supposed, law of nature, and therefore
maximally improbable. It is this maximal improbability that the weight of
the testimony would have to overcome. . . . We can now put together the
various parts of our argument. Where there is some plausible testimony
about the occurrence of what would appear to be a miracle, those who accept this as a miracle have the double burden of showing both that the event
took place and that it violated the laws of nature. But it will be very hard to
sustain this double burden. For whatever tends to show that it would have
been a violation of natural law tends for that very reason to make it most
unlikely that it actually happened. . . . [F]or this very reason there is a very
strong presumption against its having happened, which it is most unlikely
that any testimony will be able to outweigh.[1]

---

[1] Mackie, *Miracle of Theism*, 25–26.

Mackie is of course thinking of a *miracle* in the way which we looked at earlier, as being, as he puts it in one place, "an event which would not have happened in the course of nature, and which came about only through a supernatural intrusion."[2] For Mackie, a miracle is a violation of (is an exception to) a law of nature (that is, it is an exception to a *way* "in which the world . . . works when left to itself, when not interfered with"), produced by "a supernatural intrusion" into nature. But all that matters for present purposes is the first part of this, that a miracle is a violation of a law of nature, for from this Mackie infers that a miracle must be, in some sense, "maximally improbable." Since Mackie does not require that laws be true, this notion of a miracle as being "a violation of natural law" produces, of course, no a priori demonstration that there are no miracles. I do require that laws be true, but also am not beset by any such a priori demonstration, since I take a miracle to be a violation of an *apparent* law of nature. Since 'apparent law of nature' means, basically (setting aside the indexing to a person and a time), exceedingly well established, relative to a body of inductive evidence, as being a law of nature (in my sense of 'law of nature'), and since Mackie himself says that the notion on the table is "the notion of a well-established law of nature," I think that I can present his view in a way that captures its essence using my own notion of 'miracle', and shall do so.

Why, exactly, should we suppose that it is "most unlikely" that the testimony in favor of a miracle "will be able to outweigh" the inductive evidence which indeed supports exceedingly well an apparent law of nature which the occurrence of the miracle would violate? Where *m* is an alleged miracle (for us, now), allegedly witnessed (by, and only by, one person, not identical to any of us), where *L* is an apparent law which *m*'s occurrence would violate, and where *all* of our available and relevant information includes the testimony of the supposed witness, but includes nothing else which would undermine *L*, consider the following three items:

(1) In these circumstances, *L* is exceedingly probable (and *m*'s occurrence is exceedingly improbable) relative to the body of inductive evidence which supports *L*.

(2) In these circumstances, *L* is exceedingly probable (and *m*'s occurrence is exceedingly improbable) relative to all of our available and relevant information.

[2] Ibid., 22.

(3) In these circumstances, L is exceedingly probable (and m's occurrence is exceedingly improbable) simpliciter.

All that a defender of this miracle *obviously* must concede to Hume, simply in virtue of the fact that a miracle is on the table, is (1). When Mackie says that "whatever *tends to show* that it would have been a violation of natural law tends for that very reason to make it most unlikely that it actually happened" (my emphasis), he seems to suggest that we are somehow obliged to move from (1) to (2) and/or (3).

Consider first the case of (3). We do, I presume, wish to speak of probabilities and improbabilities simpliciter, as when we say that *probably* (simpliciter) the sun will rise tomorrow, and when we say that the oxygen atoms all collecting in the corner of the room so that we suffocate is *unlikely to happen*, period. (We certainly at least *talk* this way.) But I hold that such propositions as (3) are synonymous to such propositions as (2)—or, more generally, that claims of probability or improbability simpliciter are synonymous to claims of probability or improbability relative to *all* of the available and relevant information. This general principle I call *holism*. Holism seems obviously correct (what else could (3) possibly mean?), and Mackie seems to endorse it. He speaks approvingly of the "principle of accepting whatever hypothesis gives the best overall explanation of all the available and relevant evidence," and says that "the likelihood or unlikelihood, the epistemic probability or improbability, is always relative to some body of information, and may change if additional information comes in." [3] So we may now forget about (3) and concentrate on Mackie's proposed move from (1) to (2). When he says that "whatever tends to show that it would have been a violation of natural law tends for that very reason to make it most unlikely that it actually happened," I take it that he is saying that given (1) we are somehow obliged to accept (2). Now, how are we so obliged?

Though there is no known way of explaining the *general* notion of "formal implication," there nonetheless presumably is some such notion. Although the conclusion 'John is unmarried' is entailed (necessitated) separately by each of the premises 'The sky is blue and if the sky is blue then John is unmarried' and 'John is a bachelor', it presumably follows, in some "formal" way, from the first but not from the second. In any event, inasmuch as we understand the notion of formal implication, (2) obviously

[3] Ibid., 23.

does not formally follow from (1), so that cannot be the reason why we are obliged to move from (1) to (2).

It might still be asserted that (1) *entails* (necessitates or metaphysically implies) (2); that is, that it is metaphysically impossible for (1) to be true while (2) is false. But, *in the first place*, if such an assertion is made, it wants an argument. Since the available and relevant information includes (as it would be utterly tendentious and question-begging to deny) the testimony of the witness who claims to have observed the occurrence of *m*, to say that (1) entails (2) is to say that *L* is perforce exceedingly probable, and *m*'s occurrence exceedingly improbable, even relative to information which includes such testimony—that the testimony of this one witness cannot evidentially outweigh the inductive evidence which so strongly supports *L*. But *why* should we believe that? This is the very issue on the table, since the assertion that (1) entails (2) is not interestingly different from the assertion of (H) itself.

In fact, though, and *in the second place*, I think that it is rather clear that (1) does not entail (2). Consider an analogy, one that is interesting to think about in its own right. Suppose we have an exceedingly large urn, which we know to contain trillions of marbles. Suppose that we are able to sample marbles from many different regions of the urn. Let the sample be exceedingly large, though far from exhaustive; let it be as wide-ranging as we like; let us be able to conduct experiments by deliberately choosing some hitherto unexplored region of the urn to sample; or let the sampling be random, or whatever seems best. Suppose that all the very many marbles hitherto observed are green, strongly inductively supporting the hypothesis that all the marbles in the urn are green. Is this case not like (1)? The vast urn is the universe. 'All marbles in the urn are green' is an apparent "law" of this universe, one exceedingly probable relative to the body of inductive evidence which supports it. Now, a *red* marble in the urn would be the analogue of a miracle, and there being a red marble in the urn is exceedingly improbable relative to the body of inductive evidence which so strongly supports the apparent "law" that all marbles in the urn are green.

Suppose, though, that the following further information is available. Someone who is apparently—based on a substantial independent body of information we have about him or her—trustworthy, sober, sincere, visually and otherwise capable, and so on (here let the witness be your favorite person, other than yourself, of this type), swears to us with all apparent sobriety, sincerity, seriousness, and so forth, and persists in this even at great personal cost, that he or she was able to look inside the urn on one special occasion, found a red marble inside and (taking it out) spent a long time carefully examining it in good normal light, noting its obvious and exquisite redness, and then put it back into the urn. *Must* it be exceedingly probable, relative now to *all* the available and relevant information, that all the marbles in the urn are green, and exceedingly improbable that there is at least one red marble in the urn? Suppose you are in these circumstances and have heard such testimony. Suppose you now have to *bet your life* on whether the "law" is true or the "miracle" occurred. Which way will you bet? It would greatly surprise me if very many people would feel any *necessity* to bet (or even would in fact bet) against the "miracle."

But suppose I am wrong about this. We then return to the question of whether (1) entails (2). What is the argument that it does? The claim that (1) entails (2) is essentially the same as the claim that (H) is true. In a Humean argument for (H) we ought not to be taking (H) as one of our premisses.

It might be said, not that (1) entails (2), but simply that, given (1), we *ought* to accept (2). But why ought we? Here we have simply another way of asserting the sort of Humean conclusion which is supposed to be *argued* for. If a man accepts (1) but rejects (2)—as in certain cases I do myself—we have found nothing which Hume or Mackie has to say against that man. The root idea behind Mackie's discussion, that the evidence that a supposed event *m* is a miracle must at the same time, "in the very nature of the fact" as Hume would say, be the evidence that *m* did not really happen, is a sort of Humean cliché on this topic, and is of course true. But this point is unhelpful to the Humean, since there seems to be no reason at all to suppose that this evidence that *m* did not happen cannot be *outweighed* by the testimonial evidence that *m* did happen—even when that testimonial evidence is the evidence of a solitary witness. We are still in search of a noncircular *argument* for (H).

I should now say something about Mackie's "fork":

> those who deny the occurrence of a miracle have two alternative lines of defence. One is to say that the event may have occurred, but in accordance with the laws of nature. Perhaps there were unknown circumstances that made it possible; or perhaps what were thought to be the relevant laws of nature are not strictly laws; there may be as yet unknown kinds of natural causation through which this event might have come about. The other is to say that this event would indeed have violated natural law, but that for this very reason there is a very strong presumption against its having happened,

which it is most unlikely that any testimony will be able to outweigh. Usually one of these defences will be stronger than the other. For many supposedly miraculous cures, the former will be quite a likely sort of explanation, but for such feats as the bringing back to life of those who are really dead the latter will be more likely. But the *fork*, the disjunction of these two sorts of explanation, is as a whole a very powerful reply to any claim that a miracle has been performed.[4]

The main thing I want to say about the fork is that its second prong seems not to exist, save as a bare assertion, and so we hardly have a fork. I will put off my discussion of the remaining prong until our later consideration of a similar idea in John Stuart Mill.

---

[4] Ibid., 26.

[5]

Hume's Argument as Reconstructed by John Stuart Mill

Here is how Mill expounds Hume's argument:

His argument is: The evidence of miracles consists of testimony. The ground of our reliance on testimony is our experience that certain conditions being supposed, testimony is generally veracious. But the same experience tells us that even under the best conditions testimony is frequently either intentionally or unintentionally, false. When, therefore, the fact to which testimony is produced is one the happening of which would be more at variance with experience than the falsehood of testimony, we ought not to believe it. And this rule all prudent persons observe in the conduct of life. Those who do not, are sure to suffer for their credulity.

Now a miracle (the argument goes on to say) is, in the highest possible degree, contradictory to experience: for if it were not contradictory to experience it would not be a miracle. The very reason for its being regarded as a miracle is that it is a breach of a law of nature, that is, of an otherwise invariable and inviolable uniformity in the succession of natural events. There is, therefore, the very strongest reason for disbelieving it, that experience can give for disbelieving anything. But the mendacity or error of witnesses, even though numerous and of fair character, is quite within the bounds of even common experience. That supposition, therefore, ought to be preferred.[1]

[1] John Stuart Mill, *Three Essays on Religion: Nature, the Utility of Religion, and Theism,* 2d ed. (London: Longmans, Green, Reader, and Dyer, 1874), 219–220.

I will refer to the preceding as the "First Passage." Mill then says that there are "two apparently weak points in this argument," the second of which will remind the reader of the passage I earlier quoted from C. S. Lewis:

> One is, that the evidence of experience to which its appeal is made is only negative evidence, which is not so conclusive as positive; since facts of which there had been no previous experience are often discovered, and proved by positive experience to be true. The other seemingly vulnerable point is this. The argument has the appearance of assuming that the testimony of experience against miracles is undeviating and indubitable, as it would be if the whole question was about the probability of future miracles, none having taken place in the past; whereas the very thing asserted on the other side is that there have been miracles, and that the testimony of experience is not wholly on the negative side. All the evidence alleged in favour of any miracle ought to be reckoned as counter evidence in refutation of the ground on which it is asserted that miracles ought to be disbelieved. The question can only be stated fairly as depending on a balance of evidence: a certain amount of positive evidence in favour of miracles, and a negative presumption from the general course of human experience against them.[2]

I will refer to the preceding as the "Second Passage." Mill then says:

> In order to support the argument under this double correction, it has to be shown that the negative presumption against a miracle is very much stronger than that against a merely new and surprising fact. This, however, is evidently the case. A new physical discovery even if it consists in the defeating of a well established law of nature, is but the discovery of another law previously unknown. There is nothing in this but what is familiar to our experience: we were aware that we did not know all the laws of nature, and we were aware that one such law is liable to be counteracted by others. The new phenomenon, when brought to light, is found still to depend on law; it is always exactly reproduced when the same circumstances are repeated. Its occurrence, therefore, is within the limits of variation in experience, which experience itself discloses. But a miracle, in the very fact of being a miracle, declares itself to be a supersession not of one natural law by another, but of the law which includes all others, which experience shows to be universal

[2] Ibid., 220–221. The remark about the "two apparently weak points" immediately precedes the given passage.

for all phenomena, viz., that they depend on some law; that they are always the same when there are the same phenomenal antecedents, and neither take place in the absence of their phenomenal causes, nor ever fail to take place when the phenomenal conditions are all present.[3]

I will refer to the preceding as the "Third Passage." Now, let us first attend to the first 'therefore' in the First Passage. We have the argument:

(A) "The evidence of miracles consists of testimony."
(B) "The ground of our reliance on testimony is our experience that certain conditions being supposed, testimony is generally veracious."
(C) "But the same experience tells us that even under the best conditions testimony is frequently either intentionally or unintentionally, false."

Therefore

(D) "When . . . the fact to which testimony is produced is one the happening of which would be more at variance with experience than the falsehood of testimony, we ought not to believe it."

I am tempted to begin by joking that this argument is one of those which Hume said he did not understand, whose premisses say what is and whose conclusion contains "an *ought not*," and then to request an explanation "for what seems altogether inconceivable, how this new relation can be a deduction from others, which are entirely different from it."[4] But that would be, I suppose, merely joking, since presumably (B), and I suppose also (A), are normative claims of some sort.

Nevertheless, it is a serious question how (D) is supposed to follow from the premisses. Despite the obscurity of the *general* notion of "formal implication," it seems obvious enough that (D) does not in any sense formally follow from (A)–(C). (Symbolize them and see.) Formally, at least, we seem to have a non sequitur. And if the argument is an enthymeme, it is not very obvious what the intended additional premisses are. ('If (A) and (B) and (C) then (D)' would do the trick, but we might then wonder why we are obliged to believe this conditional. The reader who tries to convert

<hr>

[3] Ibid., 221–222.
[4] Hume, *Treatise of Human Nature*, 469.

the above into a *formally valid* argument with compelling premisses will learn the hidden difficulties here.)

If it is claimed simply that the premisses entail the conclusion, this claim wants a justification. It certainly might be doubted. Consider an analogy. The evidence that it will snow on June 1 in Manhattan is the report of the Weather Bureau. The ground of our reliance on reports of the Weather Bureau is our experience that, "certain conditions being supposed," reports of the Weather Bureau are generally veracious. But "the same experience" tells us, let us suppose, that reports of the Weather Bureau are "even under the best conditions" often false. Does it follow, even of necessity, that if the fact (which the report of the Weather Bureau alleges) is one the happening of which would be "more at variance" with experience than the falsehood of a report of the Weather Bureau—as I suppose such a one as this would be—then we ought not to believe the report of the Weather Bureau? I don't see how. The authors of the report are in rather a better position to know about this sort of thing than I am, and this fact does not seem to be irrelevant. (Just as Moses was in rather a better position to note whether the Sea of Reeds parted, than I am.)

And even if (D) somehow "followed" from (A)–(C), (C) is not at all obviously true, given the unclarity of "even under the best conditions." Suppose that the *best* condition is when the testimony is *true*; then, of course, it is never false "under the best conditions." Or suppose that by "the best conditions" we mean when the testimony concerns a matter of great importance and is given by a seemingly serious, capable, honorable, sober, sincere witness, who would not have been subject to punishment if not making the claim and who indeed persists in the claim even at great personal cost, and is never known to recant, *and* the testimony concerns very salient and very gross empirical matters (such as whether a visible and tangible elephant was in the living room, or whether a sea parted), *and* the testimony is based on observation apparently made carefully, thoroughly, and over a period of, say, several hours. Now, when has testimony given under *these* conditions ever been discovered to be false? Setting aside the contested cases of reports of the miraculous, the falsehood of such testimony as this would seem to be utterly "at variance with experience." The "mendacity or error of witnesses" of *this* sort (which is, of course, the relevant sort) is—setting aside the reports of miracles, as of course we must lest we beg the question—not only not "within the bounds of even common experience," but apparently utterly unknown. The strength of at least some of those miracles which are taken as the foundation of, say, Christianity or Judaism is that they are based on testimony of just this kind.

Nonetheless, Mill may say, there is "the very strongest reason for disbelieving" the miracle report "that experience can give for disbelieving anything," since the miracle would be "a breach of [an apparent] law of nature, that is, of an otherwise invariable and inviolable [observed] uniformity in the succession of natural events," so that the evidence in favor of the miracle at least *cannot outweigh* the evidence against it. But we have addressed this sort of point in our discussion of Mackie. Setting aside the problem which troubled Hume's own argument (which Mill is well aware of), all that is obvious here is that the miracle has an extreme "antecedent improbability" (Mill's words),[5] relative to the inductive evidence that so strongly supports the apparent law or uniformity. What is the Humean *argument* that the miracle is at all unlikely relative to *all* of our available and relevant information (which includes, of course, the testimony to the miracle)? Mill thus far has given no such argument.

Mill's Humean argument thus *seems* to break down at the very beginning, in a now familiar way. When in the Second Passage Mill speaks of "a negative presumption" against a miracle "from the general course of human experience," I take it that he has in mind the general course of human experience *excluding* the testimony in favor of (and the issue of the occurrence of) the alleged miracle, lest he beg the question. Now, for any such alleged miracle *m* it is perhaps obvious (setting aside the complication of *other* miracles attested to in "the general course of human experience") that:

> (E)   *m*'s occurrence is exceedingly unlikely (*m* has, as Mill sometimes says, an extreme "antecedent improbability") relative to the general course of human experience excluding the testimony to *m*.

It in no obvious way follows from (E) that:

> (F)   *m*'s occurrence is exceedingly unlikely relative to all of our available and relevant information (including the testimony to *m*).

---

[5] Mill, 228.

But (F) is what Mill needs. (F) might be *expressed* as:

> (G) *m*'s occurrence is exceedingly unlikely (there is a very strong "nega-
> tive presumption" against *m*'s occurrence) relative to "the general
> course of human experience" (where this now means relative to *all* of
> our available and relevant information).

And, given holism, (F) and (G) might be expressed as:

> (J) *m*'s occurrence is exceedingly unlikely (there is a very strong "nega-
> tive presumption" against *m*'s occurrence) simpliciter.

But even if (E) is obvious, neither (F) nor (G) nor (J) at all obviously follows from it, or is in any obvious way supported by it. The claim that,
given (E), we are obliged to accept (F), or (G), or (J), is the very claim for
which the Humean is supposed to be arguing.

Given this crucial missing step (which Mill thus far has not supplied), the
question of the *strength* of the "negative presumption," which Mill begins
to address in the Third Passage, is irrelevant. For if by the negative presumption we mean one relative to that general course of human experience which *excludes* the testimony to *m*, let it be as strong as we please—
(F) still does not follow (or we must be told how it "follows"). And if by
the negative presumption we mean one relative to that general course of
human experience which *includes* the testimony to *m*, we wish to be told
why there is here any *negative* "presumption" at all. (If the testimony is ex-
cluded, there is a mysterious and unsupported move; if the testimony is included, there is a begging of the question. Perhaps what the Humean is
trying to do is in fact impossible.)

We must now address the etherealization of the argument in terms of
"the law which includes all others," broached in the Third Passage. Mill allows, in the Second Passage, that "facts of which there had been no pre-
vious experience are often discovered, and proved by positive experience
to be true." Because of this, he says in the Third Passage that "it has to be
shown that the negative presumption against a miracle is very much
stronger than that against a merely new and surprising fact." He then adds:
"This, however, is evidently the case." How so? "A new physical discovery even if it consists in the defeating of a well established law of nature, is
but the discovery of another law previously unknown." This may sound

odd. When the Photoelectric Effect was discovered, was that discovery the "discovery of another law previously unknown," or even the discovery *that there is* "another law previously unknown"? It might seem that the absence—for all anyone knew, the eternal absence—of a new law on the table was the very reason for all the angst back then, and that the "discovery of another law" came later. And so one might wonder why, if it was right to believe in the existence of the *anomaly* in the absence of a suitable law, it is not right to believe that the Sea of Reeds parted, in the absence of a suitable law. But Mill's meaning becomes clear when he says: "The new phenomenon, when brought to light, is found still to depend on law; it is always exactly reproduced when the same circumstances are repeated." He means that that *sort* of phenomenon has been observed more than once, always attendant on the same *natural* circumstances—which certainly distinguishes the Photoelectric Effect from the parting of the Sea of Reeds, however obscure 'the same' and 'natural' may be. Mill then says:

> But a miracle, in the very fact of being a miracle, declares itself to be a supersession not of one natural law by another, but of the law which includes all others, which experience shows to be universal for all phenomena, viz., that they depend on some law; that they are always the same when there are the same phenomenal antecedents, and neither take place in the absence of their phenomenal causes, nor ever fail to take place when the phenomenal conditions are all present.

I will refer to this as the "Curious Passage."

It is not obvious what Mill means by 'miracle', and the question of what he means is crucial since, as we will see, all that is novel in Mill's argument—all that goes beyond Hume or Mackie—turns on the peculiarly Millian notion of what a miracle is. In the First Passage, where Mill was expounding Hume, the idea seemed to be ("The very reason for its being regarded as a miracle . . .") that a miracle is "a breach of a law of nature, that is, of an otherwise invariable and inviolable uniformity in the succession of natural events." (Note, by the way, the interesting word 'otherwise'. This is already a Millian modification of Hume. Note also that this may be—and indeed is, as we will see—simply Mill's corrected version of one of Hume's definitions of 'miracle', not Mill's own.) In the Curious Passage, however, it seems to be part of the notion of a miracle that it is not subsumable under any such "law of nature," known or unknown. Later in his discussion, Mill says:

> When we say that an ordinary physical fact always takes place according to some invariable law, we mean that it is connected by uniform sequence or coexistence with some definite set of physical antecedents; that whenever that set is exactly reproduced the same phenomenon will take place, unless counteracted by the similar laws of some other physical antecedents; and that whenever it does take place, it would always be found that its special set of antecedents (or one of its sets if it has more than one) has pre-existed. Now, an event which takes place in this manner, is not a miracle. To make it a miracle it must be produced by a direct volition, without the use of means; or at least, of any means which if simply repeated would produce it. To constitute a miracle a phenomenon must take place without having been preceded by any antecedent phenomenal conditions sufficient again to reproduce it; or a phenomenon for the production of which the antecedent conditions existed, must be arrested or prevented without the intervention of any phenomenal antecedents which would arrest or prevent it in a future case. The test of a miracle is: Were there present in the case such external conditions, such second causes we may call them, that whenever these conditions or causes reappear the event will be reproduced? If there were, it is not a miracle; if there were not, it is a miracle, but it is not according to law: it is an event produced, without, or in spite of law.[6]

Even in this passage it is not completely clear what the proposed definition of 'miracle' is. On the one hand, the notion seems to be *volitional*: a miracle is an event produced by a *direct* volition of some agent (not necessarily, I take it, divine), that is, "without the use of means; or at least, of any means which if simply repeated [that is, minus the volition] would produce it." On the other hand, at the end of the passage a miracle seems to be simply "an event produced, without, or in spite of law"—which might seem to suggest that whatever is truly anomalous is a miracle: "if there were not . . . present in the case such external conditions, such second causes we may call them, that whenever these conditions or causes reappear the event will be reproduced . . . it is a miracle." Does Mill really mean that *any* event which has no "second causes" is a miracle, whether produced by a volition or not? What, then, of: "To make it a miracle it must be produced by a di-

---

[6] Ibid., 224–225.

rect volition . . . .''? But perhaps Mill is assuming that "the case" mentioned above involves an alleged event of allegedly volitional origin. We may note that, at the end of the final sentence, Mill does not say that a miracle is an event which *occurs* "without, or in spite of law," but one which is thus *produced*. And perhaps Mill means that the miracle must be produced not just by something, but by a volition of an agent. Given his later remarks (which we will look at), which place special emphasis on the volitional origin of a miracle, I will suppose that for Mill a miracle is an event produced "without, or in spite of law" by a volition of some agent. For the main issue which concerns us, it does not matter whether we adopt this Millian definition of 'miracle', or take the Millian notion to be simply that of an event which occurs "without, or in spite of law." The important point is that a Millian miracle has no "second causes"—it is a phenomenon not tied to other phenomena in a web of phenomenal regularity—and thus violates "the law which includes all others." (I am not sure whether the notion that a miracle is "a breach of a law of nature" is supposed now to be—somehow—a *consequence* of the above, or is simply left behind.)

In any event, we have a rough idea of what a Millian miracle is. Now, what is the Millian argument against the acceptability of my believing, supposing I should want to, in the occurrence of Millian miracles (that God, say, produced by "a direct volition" the parting of the Sea of Reeds—the "strong east wind"[7] being a *means*, but not a means "which if simply repeated would produce" such a parting; *or* the wind being "sufficient" for the parting, but *its* production being the miracle)? Let us grant, as Mill says in the Curious Passage (reading 'miracle' as 'Millian miracle'), that a Millian miracle "declares itself to be a supersession not of one natural law by another, but of the law which includes all others . . . [that] all phenomena . . . depend on some [natural] law; that they are always the same when there are the same phenomenal antecedents, and neither take place in the absence of their phenomenal causes, nor ever fail to take place when the phenomenal conditions are all present." In the Curious Passage, Mill says that "experience shows" us that "the law which includes all others" is true. Thereafter, in discussing "this argument against belief in miracles," he implies that "the universal dependence of phenomena on invariable laws" is "a scientifically established truth,"[8] and says that "in the progress of sci-

---

[7] Exodus 14:21.
[8] Mill, 222.

ence, all phenomena have been shown, by indisputable evidence, to be amenable to law, and even in the cases in which those laws have not yet been exactly ascertained, delay in ascertaining them is fully accounted for by the special difficulties of the subject."[9]

One might wonder how, if in Mill's own day there were "cases in which those laws have not yet been exactly ascertained" owing to "the special difficulties of the subject," he could justly assert that "all phenomena have been shown, by indisputable evidence, to be amenable to law," but I take it that Mill is making an induction on the success of science. Look, he is saying, all of *these* hitherto explored phenomena are phenomena which are shown in the fullness of time to be amenable to natural law (because they already have become so amenable), hence all phenomena are phenomena which are shown in the fullness of time to be amenable to natural law. There is another passage in this vein:

> [Even] assuming as a fact the existence and providence of God, the whole of our observation of Nature proves to us by incontrovertible evidence that the rule of his government is by means of second causes; that all facts, or at least all physical facts, follow uniformly upon given physical conditions, and never occur but when the appropriate collection of physical conditions is realized. . . . This was not obvious in the infancy of science; it was more and more recognized as the processes of nature were more carefully and accurately examined, until there now remains no class of phenomena of which it is not positively known, save some cases which from their obscurity and complication our scientific processes have not yet been able completely to clear up and disentangle, and in which, therefore, the proof that they also are governed by natural laws could not, in the present state of science, be more complete. The evidence, though merely negative, which these circumstances afford that government by second causes is universal, is admitted for all except directly religious purposes to be conclusive. When either a man of science for scientific or a man of the world for practical purposes inquires into an event, he asks himself what is its cause? and not, has it any natural cause? A man would be laughed at who set down as one of the alternative suppositions that there is no other cause for it than the will of God.[10]

Let us begin with two minor points. Note, only to set aside, the reappearance here of—or at least an apparently approving acknowledgment

[9] Ibid., 223.
[10] Ibid., 233–234.

of—what I thought Socrates had forever discouraged in philosophy: refutation by laughter. And note the curious ambiguity in the phrase "could not, in the present state of science, be more complete," between a meritorious, superlative sense of "could not . . . be more complete," and a more appropriate (and doubtless intended) less meritorious sense. The evidence for the existence of microorganisms in the Andromeda Galaxy could not, in the present state of science, be more complete, but we ought not to be concluding anything about the universality of microorganisms. Why, given the incompletion of which Mill speaks, should we be concluding that "government by second causes is universal"? Why is Mill's induction on the success of science a *reasonable* induction to make?

More fundamentally, suppose we make our now familiar objection. Suppose that someone claims to have observed a Millian miracle *m*. Does the experience which "shows" us that "all phenomena [are] . . . amenable to [natural] law" include the testimony to *m*, or not? If it does, the claim that that experience "shows" us that all phenomena are amenable to natural law begs the question. (Why is "the law which includes all others" reasonably inferred from experience which includes such testimony?) If it does not, then there is the unanswered question of how we get from the fact (supposing it is a fact) that this highest law is exceedingly probable relative to that experience, to the desired conclusion that this highest law is exceedingly probable relative to all of our available and relevant information, which is—does anyone dispute it?—the only proper experiential guide to what we should believe. (Again, there is the faint suggestion of the sheer impossibility of the Humean's task.)

It is here that Mill makes an interesting move against the above argument (that argument seemingly so perfect and complete). The move I take to be that of saying that no one could reasonably claim, in our actual circumstances, to have *observed* a (Millian) miracle. The passage is worth quoting at length.

divine interference with nature could be proved if we had the same sort of evidence for it which we have for human interferences. The question of antecedent improbability only arises because divine interposition is not certified by the direct evidence of perception, but is always a matter of inference, and more or less of speculative inference. And a little consideration will show that in these circumstances the antecedent presumption against the truth of the inference is extremely strong. . . . Divine interference, by hypothesis . . . produces its effect without means, or with such as are in

themselves insufficient. . . . [T]he event is supposed not to have been produced at all through physical causation, while there is no direct evidence to
connect it with any volition. The ground on which it is ascribed to a volition is only negative, because there is no other apparent way of accounting
for its existence.

But in this merely speculative explanation there is always another hypothesis possible, viz., that the event may have been produced by physical
causes, in a manner not apparent. It may either be due to a law of physical
nature not yet known, or to the unknown presence of the conditions necessary for producing it according to some known law. . . . [S]o long . . . as
the miraculous character of the event is but an inference from the supposed
inadequacy of the laws of physical nature to account for it, so long will the
hypothesis of a natural origin for the phenomenon be entitled to preference
over that of a supernatural one. The commonest principles of sound judgment forbid us to suppose for any effect a cause of which we have absolutely
no experience, unless all those of which we have experience are ascertained
to be absent. . . . [W]hen we hear of a prodigy we always, in these modern
times, believe that if it really occurred it was neither the work of God nor
of a demon, but the consequence of some unknown natural law or of some
hidden fact. Nor is either of these suppositions precluded when, as in the
case of a miracle properly so called, the wonderful event seemed to depend
upon the *will* of a human being. [My emphasis.] It is always possible that
there may be at work some undetected law of nature which the wonderworker may have acquired, consciously or unconsciously, the power of calling into action; or that the wonder may have been wrought (as in the truly
extraordinary feats of jugglers) by the employment, unperceived by us, of
ordinary laws: which also need not necessarily be a case of voluntary de-
ception; or, lastly, the event may have had no connection with the volition
at all, but the coincidence between them may be the effect of craft or acci-
dent, the miracle-worker having seemed or affected to produce by his will
that which was already about to take place, as if one were to command an
eclipse of the sun at the moment when one knew by astronomy that an
eclipse was on the point of taking place. In a case of this description, the
miracle might be tested by a challenge to repeat it; but it is worthy of remark, that recorded miracles were seldom or never put to this test. No
miracle-worker seems ever to have made a *practice* of raising the dead: that
and the other most signal of the miraculous operations are reported to have
been performed only in one or a few isolated cases, which may have been
either cunningly selected cases, or accidental coincidences. There is, in
short, nothing to exclude the supposition that every alleged miracle was due
to natural causes: and as long as that supposition remains possible, no scientific observer, and no man of ordinary practical judgment, would assume

by conjecture a cause which no reason existed for supposing to be real, save the necessity of accounting for something which is sufficiently accounted for without it. . . . The existence of God cannot possibly be proved by miracles, for unless a God is already recognized, the apparent miracle can always be accounted for on a more probable hypothesis than that of the interference of a Being of whose very existence it is supposed to be the sole evidence.[11]

I will refer to this as the "Mysterious Passage."

The situation now clarifies itself. I find no good argument in Mill for (H), where in (H) 'miracle' is taken in my sense, not a Millian miracle. For I find no good argument in Mill (or in Mackie or in Hume) against the perfect rationality of my believing in the observable physical occurrences reported below, though the report be that of a solitary witness. With Mill's discussion in mind, let us for now overlook the reference to Yahweh's causal activity, and concentrate solely on such aspects of these alleged events as would have been observable by the supposed witness (whose testimony I believe for *historical* reasons we have either directly or almost so —this is a complicated matter which I cannot go into here; for the sake of the philosophical discussion, assume that we have firsthand testimony by a supposed eyewitness).[12]

Stretched out Moses his hand over the sea, and caused to go Yahweh the sea by a wind of the east, strong, all night; and he made the sea for dry land, and were divided the waters. And came the children of Israel into the midst of the sea on dry ground; and the waters being to them a wall from their right hand and from their left hand.[13]

And Aaron lifted up the staff, and smote the water which was in the river before the eyes of Pharaoh, and before the eyes of his servants; and was turned all the water which was in the river to blood. And the fish which

---

[11] Ibid., 228–232.

[12] On these historical matters see, for example, Gleason Archer, *A Survey of Old Testament Introduction*, 3d ed. (Chicago: Moody Press, 1994); F. F. Bruce, *The New Testament Documents: Are They Reliable?* (Grand Rapids, Mich.: Eerdmans, 1967); and W. F. Albright and C. S. Mann, *Matthew* (Garden City, N.Y.: Doubleday, 1971), especially clxxvii–clxxxvi.

[13] Exodus 14:21–22; from George Ricker Berry, *The Interlinear Literal Translation of the Hebrew Old Testament* (Grand Rapids, Mich.: Kregel Publications, 1970), 281. (This is a reprint of the 1897 Hinds and Noble edition.)

were in the river died, and stank the river; and were not able the Egyptians to drink water from the river; and was the blood in all the land of Egypt.[14]

Now in the fourth watch of the night he came toward them walking on the sea. And the disciples seeing him on the sea walking were troubled saying, "A phantasm [*phantasma*] it is," and from fear they cried out. But immediately spoke Jesus to them saying: "Be of good cheer. I am [*egō eimi*]. Do not fear." And answering him Peter said: "Lord, if thou art, command me to come to thee on the waters." And he said: "Come." And going down from the ship Peter walked on the waters and came toward Jesus. But seeing the wind he was afraid, and beginning to sink he cried out saying "Lord, save me." And immediately Jesus stretching out his hand took hold of him, and says to him: "Little-faith [*oligopiste*], why didst thou doubt?" And as they went up into the ship, ceased the wind. And the ones in the ship worshipped him saying: "Truly thou art the Son of God."[15]

When it was early evening on that day, the first of the week, and the doors having been shut where the disciples were because of fear of the Jews, came Jesus and stood in the midst, and says to them: "Peace to you." And saying this he showed his hands and his side to them. Then were the disciples glad, when they saw the Lord.[16]

And as they said these things he stood in the midst of them. But scared and becoming terrified they thought a spirit to behold. And he said to them: "Why are you troubled, and why do thoughts come up in your hearts? See my hands and my feet, that I am myself; feel me and see, because a spirit has not flesh and bones as you behold me having." And while they yet believed not for joy, and marveled, he said to them: "Have you any food here?" And they handed to him part of a broiled fish; and taking it, before them he ate.[17]

Such of these reported physical occurrences as would have been observable by the witnesses I believe in very truth to have occurred, and I believe this on the testimony of those witnesses. Nor have we found any good philo-

[14] Exodus 7:20–21; in Berry, 246–247.

[15] Matthew 14:25–33; from Alfred Marshall, *The Interlinear Greek-English New Testament* (London: Samuel Bagster and Sons, 1958).

[16] John 20:19–20; from Marshall, except for the final sentence, which is from the King James translation.

[17] Luke 24:36–43; mostly from Marshall.

sophical argument for the claim that I ought not so to believe. Now, if it should turn out that there simply is no such argument against the rationality of crediting such testimony—which will be the case if there is no good philosophical argument for (H)—this will surely be a source of surprise to the philosophical community, whether the physical occurrences be *Millian* miracles or not.

Concerning the Mysterious Passage (in which Mill argues that no collection of miracles, in my sense, can ever be compelling evidence for a theological theory), I will at present say only two things. First, Mill claims that the "commonest principles of sound judgment forbid us to suppose for any effect a cause of which we have absolutely no experience, unless all those of which we have experience are ascertained to be absent." But, given what he says earlier in the passage, "ascertained to be absent" must be taken in rather a strong sense, since it is allowed that the effect "may either be due to a law of physical nature not yet known, or to the unknown presence of the conditions necessary for producing it according to some known law." But how then is this "principle of sound judgment" followed even in science? When Enrico Fermi (following Wolfgang Pauli) [18] postulated the existence of "a cause of which we [had] absolutely no experience"—the neutrino (the "little neutral one")—to explain a certain effect (Beta decay), how had he "ascertained" that the then familiar particles were not *somehow* producing the effect by way of "a law of physical nature not yet known"? How is it that he rightly postulated the existence of an otherwise unknown cause, rather than postulate the existence of otherwise unknown *powers* of the familiar particles? Fermi was of course perfectly justified, but it will be very difficult for Mill to explain why. In science, there are always logically possible alternative hypotheses for explaining any effect, especially if we are given a free hand vis-à-vis "a law of physical nature not yet known, or . . . the unknown presence of the conditions necessary for producing it according to some known law." The explainer who is free with *law* and free with *conditions* is free indeed. So how will we ever get to the neutrino?

Of course, Fermi's explanation was somehow *better* than the (ever-present) logically possible alternatives, in a way philosophers of science find hard to specify. It was *simpler*, or more *natural* (which of course does not

---

[18] For some of the details, see, for example, Hans Frauenfelder and Ernest M. Henley, *Subatomic Physics*, 2d ed. (Englewood Cliffs, N.J.: Prentice Hall, 1991), 310–312.

mean "natural" in Mill's sense) than its gerrymandered competitors (which were equally "natural" in Mill's sense). But if considerations of "simplicity" or of "naturalness" (or, as one sometimes hears, of "beauty" or "the ring of truth"), whatever these may mean exactly, can give preference to one scientific explanation over (at least) its gerrymandered competitors, why might not such considerations give preference to a theological or supernatural explanation over its gerrymandered naturalistic competitors? When Mill says that the "existence of God cannot possibly be proved by miracles," this is, taken in a certain sense, perhaps trivially true, given what Mill means by 'miracle'. But then the claim is hardly significant. More to the point is the question of whether the existence of God can be proved by miracles (in my sense)—by those extraordinary physical occurrences such as the parting of or walking on a sea, or the reappearance, vigorously alive, of those who recently had been crucified, spear-pierced, and entombed—the *happening* of which Mill has given us no reason at all to dispute. Why might not the best explanation of such a miracle be a theological or supernatural explanation? Mill needs to say why this *cannot* be so, without invoking over-strong and implausible and unsupported "principles of sound judgment."

For my own part I do not see why the same sort of considerations (of "simplicity," "naturalness," etc.) which properly lead one to explain a certain physical effect in terms of the existence of an otherwise unknown entity, a neutrino (rather than in terms of unknown logically possible powers of familiar particles), *might* not also properly lead one to explain a certain physical effect in terms of the existence of an otherwise unknown intelligent and powerful entity, a deity (rather than in terms of unknown logically possible powers of natural objects). As for Mill's remark that a miracle "might be tested by a challenge to repeat it," I don't see how *repetition* is relevant to the point now at issue. Repetition, if relevant to anything, is relevant to the question of the reality of the effect, not (in any obvious way) to its explanation. But the reality of the *physical effect* is at present being taken for granted. (If Mill is here taking up again the earlier discussion, and now wants to claim that testimony to unrepeated extraordinary physical effects should not be given credence, such a claim is in need of the very sort of cogent Humean argument which we have not found in Mill.) If the claim is that, in the absence of repetition, *coincidence* is a logically possible "explanation" of the effect, that (if it is an explanation at all) remains logically possible after ever so many repetitions. If the claim is that, in the absence of repetition, coincidence must always be at least as plausible an explanation of the effect as is any supernatural explanation, that claim wants an argument.

Perhaps Mill is assuming (as *perhaps* Hume holds in the *Dialogues concerning Natural Religion*—but see the remarkable third dialogue and the rejoinder there by Cleanthes, which Philo never answers)[19] that a *single, unique* physical event can never, as it were, demand an explanation other than coincidence. This is far from being obvious. Suppose that in England there is an enormous billiard table, ten thousand million square feet in area. Racked up on this table in random order are one thousand million billiard balls labeled from '1' to '1,000,000,000'. There is also a massive cue ball and an enormous and powerful "cue stick," with which the balls will be "broken." Suppose that for political or financial reasons this can only be done once. So there is a single physical event, unique of its kind: the Big Break. Suppose, further, that the table's surface is divided into ten thousand million little squares, each one square foot in area, and each bearing the name of some natural number from 0 to 9, with one thousand million of each of these ten kinds, and these randomly distributed over the surface. The Big Break occurs. We find that the ball labeled '1' lands on a square labeled '1', the ball labeled '2' lands on a square labeled '4', the ball labeled '3' lands on a square labeled '1', the ball labeled '4' lands on a square labeled '5', and so forth, spelling out the first one thousand million digits of π after the decimal point. Would not the Big Break, though unique, cry out for some explanation other than coincidence?

My second remark about the Mysterious Passage will be brief. It is just a little story. Recall the account from the fourteenth chapter of *Matthew*, about Jesus walking on the sea. Suppose that Mill and I have gone back in time and are sitting discreetly in the boat. In the fourth watch of the night comes Jesus walking on the sea. Peter goes out, takes a few steps, and then begins to sink. Jesus rescues him and the two get into the boat; then some or all of the disciples say to Jesus, "Surely you are the Son of God." I say to Mill that I quite agree with them. Mill then turns to me and says: "Look, whatever these ignorant and incompetent people may say, you—as a man

---

[19] Hume, *Dialogues concerning Natural Religion*, edited by Norman Kemp Smith (Indianapolis: Bobbs-Merrill, 1947), part III, 152–155.

of modern times—should see that you have no evidence at all for this theological claim. You are overlooking the possibility that this business of walking on the sea was the result of conspiring unknown natural circumstances, perhaps a natural *coincidence* of some sort; or perhaps this wonderworker cunningly played on known natural laws, as in the truly extraordinary feats of jugglers."

6

Hume's Argument as Reconstructed by Antony Flew

Flew's remarks on our topic, which have been widely influential, are numerous and somewhat diffuse, but it is best to begin by letting Flew speak for himself:

> The criterion of a nomological is at the same time a criterion of reliability . . . [and] the appropriate way to test for reliability is to subject to strains. If this is correct then to be justified in asserting that some law of nature in fact obtains you must know that the appropriate nomological has been thoroughly tested for reliability, whether directly on its own account separately, or indirectly via the testing of some wider structure of theory from which it follows as a consequence. To be in this position is to be both warranted and required to employ this nomological as one of your critical canons. . . . The nomologicals which we know, or think we know, must serve as fundamental canons of our historical criticism. Finding what appears to be historical evidence for an occurrence inconsistent with such a nomological, we must always insist on interpreting that evidence in some other way: for if the nomological is true then it is physically impossible that any event incompatible with it could have occurred. . . . This might present itself as a conflict between Science and History. For on the one side we have what purports to be an historical proof: while on the other the nomological is supposed to have been established by methods which might in a very broad sense be classed as scientific. But the antagonists in this contest are unevenly matched. Certainly the historical evidence could constitute a sufficient reason for re-examining the nomological; and under this re-examination it might fail to sustain its claim to be believed. But if, on the contrary, it sur-

vived such testing then it would be rational—though of course it could always be mistaken—to reject the historical 'proof'; on the single and sufficient ground that we now have the best of reasons for insisting that what it purports to prove is in fact impossible.

The justification for giving the 'scientific' this ultimate preference here over the 'historical' lies in the nature of the propositions concerned and in the evidence which can be deployed to sustain them. . . . The candidate historical proposition will be particular, often singular, and in the past tense. . . . But just by reason of this very pastness and particularity it is no longer possible for anyone to examine the subject directly for himself. All that there is left to examine is the present detritus of the past, which includes the physical records of testimony. This detritus can be interpreted as evidence only in the light of our present knowledge, or presumed knowledge, of men and things; a category which embraces, although it is certainly not exhausted by, our stock of general nomologicals. This surely is and must always be the fundamental principle of historical interpretation.[1]

It will be helpful to look also at two other brief passages before we try to figure out what Flew is saying:

[Hume's] fundamental theses are: first, that the detritus of the past cannot be construed as any sort of historical evidence unless we presume that the same basic regularities obtained then as obtain today; and second, that in trying as best he may to determine what actually happened, the historian has to employ as criteria all his present knowledge and presumed knowledge of what is probable or improbable, possible or impossible. In the *Treatise* Hume argued that it is only upon such presumptions that we can justify even the basic conclusion that certain kinds of ink marks on old pieces of paper constitute testimonial evidence.[2]

Nomological propositions are open and general. Also they can, at least in principle, be tested for truth or falsity at any time or in any place. Precisely that is why it is reasonable and right for the critical historian to employ all available confirmed nomologicals as canons of exclusion, ruling out many

---

[1] Flew, *Hume's Philosophy of Belief*, 205–208.

[2] Flew, "The Impossibility of the Miraculous," in *Hume's Philosophy of Religion: The Sixth James Montgomery Hester Seminar* [no editor given] (Winston-Salem, N.C.: Wake Forest University Press, 1986), 21–22. A passage almost exactly identical to this appears in Flew's introduction to *Of Miracles*, by David Hume (La Salle, Ill.: Open Court, 1985), 13.

conceivable and even sometimes seemingly well-evidenced occurrences as
practically [physically] impossible.[3]

Flew's argument in these passages seems to be the following:

(F1) All now available confirmed nomologicals have survived strenuous
      testing.

(F2) All now available confirmed nomologicals are "open and general"
      and "can, at least in principle, be tested for truth or falsity at any time
      or in any place."

(F3) No historical propositions are nomologicals; they are not "open and
      general," but rather "particular, often singular, and in the past tense,"
      and because of this they cannot now or in the future be subjected to
      strenuous testing, nor can they in any obvious way "be tested for
      truth or falsity."

(F4) All historical propositions are evidentially based on "the present de-
      tritus of the past, which includes the physical records of testimony."

(F5) The "detritus of the past cannot be construed as any sort of histori-
      cal evidence unless we presume that the same basic regularities ob-
      tained then as obtain today."

Therefore:

(F6) "[I]t is reasonable and right for the critical historian to employ all
      available confirmed nomologicals as canons of exclusion."

It is a nice question how the conclusion would be supposed to follow from
the premises. The idea is perhaps something roughly like this. We first
consider a subsidiary matter which I will call the "Argument Sketch." Let
'Herodotus' name an arbitrary critical historian, and let 'N' name the set
of all those "confirmed nomologicals" now available to Herodotus. Suppose Herodotus now is confronted with an historical proposition, which
we now name 'P', about some alleged event supposedly occurring before
Herodotus was born. (F4) tells us, I suppose, that for any time t, Herodotus
rightly believes P at t only if he rightly believes at t some proposition describing what is, for Herodotus at t, part of "the detritus of the past." (F5)
tells us, I suppose, that for any time t, no proposition describing what is for

---

[3] Flew, "Impossibility of the Miraculous," 26. An almost exactly identical passage appears
in the introduction to *Of Miracles*, 18–19.

Herodotus at t part of "the detritus of the past" is rightly believed by Herodotus at t unless Herodotus rightly believes at t every member of the set of all those "confirmed nomologicals" available to Herodotus at t. Thus, Herodotus now rightly believes P only if Herodotus now rightly believes every member of N. So if P is inconsistent with N then Herodotus now rightly believes P only if the set of all those propositions now rightly believed by Herodotus is inconsistent. *Missing premiss*: No critical historian at any time is such that the set of all those propositions which he rightly believes at that time is inconsistent. Hence, if P is inconsistent with N, then it is not the case that Herodotus now rightly believes P. End of Argument Sketch. *Missing premiss*: Every critical historian appreciates the force of the Argument Sketch. *Missing premiss*: Whoever appreciates the force of the Argument Sketch is such that it is reasonable and right for him to employ all those "confirmed nomologicals" now available to him as "canons of exclusion" for any historical proposition that is inconsistent with the set of those nomologicals. Hence. . . .

No one except Flew can tell us what argument Flew has in mind, and he does not tell us, leaving us to speculate about the logical details. Such speculation is not very profitable, and I will not consider variations on, or alternatives to, the above. I leave to others also the task of assessing the plausibility of the "missing premisses" added above—which I certainly do not endorse—along with the worries about opacity attendant to the above construal of the implications of (F4) and (F5). (It is really astonishing that Flew should be so casual about the details of his own most central argument.) I will simply note that if anything like the above is the Flewian argument, then (F1)–(F3) are not directly part of it.

(F6), we should note, certainly does not follow from (F2), on any natural symbolization, contrary to what in the last passage above Flew incautiously seems to suggest: "Precisely that is why . . ." Nor does it in any discernible way follow from the fact that you know that a certain nomological "has been thoroughly [and successfully] tested for reliability" that you are "required to employ this nomological as one of your critical canons," even to the exclusion of an alleged exception to it. In such remarks, Flew is in grave danger of simply asserting the Humean claim at issue.

Perhaps (F1)–(F3) are intended somehow to support (F4) or (F5). (F3), which has been disputed by Swinburne,[4] perhaps supports (F4), but (F4) is

⁴ Swinburne, ed., *Miracles*, 142–143.

perhaps plausible enough on its own (if present memories count as part of "the present detritus of the past"). It is utterly unclear how (F1)–(F3) would support (F5), a premiss which is seriously ambiguous and which on any of its several natural readings is at best unmotivated. Flew's argument, though, in whatever plausible way it is construed, obviously turns on this crucial (F5).

I assume that it is clear that by "the same basic regularities" (or what he elsewhere calls "the same fundamental regularities")[5] Flew means *all* the same "basic regularities," rather than some or most of them. Only if he means all (as his words most naturally suggest) does he have any hope of getting to (F6), in which the 'all' is obviously crucial to the significance of the conclusion vis-à-vis the issue about miracles. (For if the critical historian is not obliged to employ all available "confirmed nomologicals" as canons of exclusion, then we have no assurance against the possibility that the alleged miracle would violate only one or more unemployed nomologicals, "History" then perhaps triumphing over "Science.") But what does Flew mean by the "basic regularities" without whose presumption the would-be construer of detritus cannot construe that detritus as historical evidence? With the desired (F6) in mind, the most natural interpretation is that these basic regularities are the "available confirmed nomologicals"—*available*, that is, to the would-be construer, to the critical historian. But what does this mean? Are the "confirmed nomologicals" now available to the critical historian simply the "confirmed nomologicals" of present science? But then if in (F5) Flew means *all* such "basic regularities," the truth of (F5) is far from obvious. Why, in construing bits of the detritus of the past as historical evidence for the proposition that *Caesar conquered Gaul*, must the critical historian presume that, say, Coulomb's law "obtained then"? (It is not very clear what Flew means by "obtained then." This would most naturally be taken simply to mean that the law is true— that it is never and nowhere violated, not even by two contemporaneous charged particles ["at rest"] in, say, the Orion Nebula. But perhaps Flew means that the law "obtained then" if and only if nothing violates it in a certain past spatiotemporal slice of the Earth.) The preceding question calls attention to an important ambiguity in (F5): What is the *content* of the required presumption? Must the critical historian have before his mind a *list*

---

[5] Gary R. Habermas and Antony G. N. Flew, *Did Jesus Rise from the Dead? The Resurrection Debate* (San Francisco: Harper and Row, 1987), 5.

of all now available "confirmed nomologicals" and believe that *this* one obtained, and *this* obtained, and so on? Such a requirement (even if the critical historian is not required to understand these items) is absurdly strong, and would put many critical historians out of business. (How many will have the law of Malus aforethought?) Or is the critical historian required only to believe a generalization: that all "confirmed nomologicals" currently available to the scientific community obtained in the past? I assume that this latter requirement is what Flew means by "presume that the same basic regularities obtained then as obtain today." But why should this generalization have to be believed in order to construe detritus as historical evidence? (Why isn't this as strange as requiring that a critical historian must recite the Nicene Creed before he can go about his work?) Perhaps a critical historian must believe (either as a generalization or particularly for each) that certain "confirmed nomologicals"—about how ink is preserved on paper, or about the chemical properties of vellum, or about human psychology or language, or some other such basic regularities directly relevant to his *construal* of detritus as historical evidence—obtained in the past. But why must he have so *general* a belief as the above? If Gibbon had declined to believe so universal a generalization of this kind (perhaps because of some anticipation of what they call "the stormy history of science"), and had even come to believe the existential assertion that some "confirmed nomological" of his day did not obtain in Roman times (because, say, it is simply false), would he then have been an historian but not a "critical" historian? Would any of his historical claims thereby have been less well-evidenced? It is hard to see why. If Hume had denied in his heart the proposition that Boyle's law obtained without exception in Elizabethan England, would the ink marks on old pieces of paper at the Advocates' Library in Edinburgh have been useless to the author of the *History of England, from the Invasion of Julius Caesar to the Revolution in 1688*?[6] I trow not.

Perhaps Flew means only that a critical historian must (in order to be able to construe detritus as historical evidence) believe that all currently available "confirmed nomologicals" relevant to the historical issue at hand obtained in the past. Now, where a miracle is alleged, the "confirmed

---

[6] This is the title later given to the collection of six volumes by Hume on the history of England, first published in 1754–62. For notes on these volumes, see David Fate Norton, ed., *The Cambridge Companion to Hume* (Cambridge: Cambridge University Press, 1993), 358–359, and David Wootton, "David Hume, 'the historian'," in the same volume, 281–312.

nomological" which it would violate is certainly in some sense relevant to the historical issue at hand. But why must the critical historian, qua critical historian, assume the truth of the *disputed* nomological, and not just the truth of those relevant nomologicals (about ink, paper, and so forth) which he perhaps more obviously needs to believe in order to construe the detritus of the past (here, "the physical records of testimony") as historical evidence? There is no apparent reason why he must always be obliged to believe the disputed nomological in order to construe the physical records as testimony to a counterinstance to that nomological. (Perhaps if, at the wedding feast in Cana, Jesus had turned the water not into wine but into *ink*, there might conceivably have been some sort of metahistorical problem here; but such will hardly in general be the case with claims to the miraculous.)

Flew occasionally hints at the following sort of retort.[7] If the critical historian accepts some of the available and relevant "confirmed nomologicals"—those whose acceptance is perhaps necessary for an act of construal—but not all of the available and relevant "confirmed nomologicals," then he is being arbitrary, which is somehow bad. But, of course, from the fact that a critical historian is being selective in his allegiance to "confirmed nomologicals," it in no way follows that he is being arbitrary. What rules out the possibility that considerations of simplicity, or naturalness, or overall historical plausibility, tell in favor of such selectivity in a certain case? I am aware that the Humean wants to *say* that this cannot happen; what is missing is the Humean argument for such an assertion.

Flew's very retort, by the way, suggests another difficulty for the demanding (F5)—and for the demanding (F6). *Might* not a desire for *consistency with present observation* force a critical historian to reject at least one of the available and relevant "confirmed nomologicals"? Suppose that before him is a *document* (say, a seeming piece of parchment seemingly bearing ink marks) observably of (so to say) type alpha, which seems to say (if the apparent ink marks are construed in the normal way) that there was once (so to speak) a beta that was not a gamma. Suppose that included among the available and relevant "confirmed nomologicals" are items of this sort:

(F7) All documents of type alpha are documents which say what they seem to say and are completely accurate.

(F8) Whatever is a beta (at a certain time) is a gamma (at that time).

---

[7] Flew, "Miracles," in *The Encyclopedia of Philosophy*, 8 vols., ed. Paul Edwards (New York: Macmillan, 1967), 5:352.

What precludes this possibility? If Flew claims that nothing like (F7) could be a "confirmed nomological," that claim wants an argument. For all we know a priori, something like (F7) might not only be testable for reliability, but indeed have been found to have survived strenuous testing—there *might* be lots of such documents still being produced and much information (as flattering as necessary) available about their content and accuracy. Who can preclude this in advance for all interpretations of 'type alpha'?

But perhaps we are still not apprehending Flew's meaning. Perhaps he has in mind that a critical historian must believe, not that all currently available "confirmed nomologicals" (nor even all such ones as are *relevant* to the historical issue at hand) obtained in the past, but rather that all (true) laws of nature ("the same basic regularities"?), confirmed or not, known or not, obtained in the past. Undoubtedly, a critical historian should believe this. But if this is the requirement prescribed in (F5), then Flew has no chance of getting to (F6); and what he could get to from this would be of no help whatsoever to any Humean argument against the credibility of the miraculous. (This is even supposing (F5) would then be *true*. Although it would be foolish of a critical historian not to believe that universal lawful regularities—laws of nature which are, or which are expressed by, universal generalizations which are true—obtain everywhere and everywhen, the incompatibility of being foolish in this way and being able to construe the detritus of the past as historical evidence is not obvious.)

Perhaps Flew means the preceding *and* that the critical historian should regard the set of "confirmed nomologicals" currently available to the scientific community as being the best guide to what the (true) laws of nature are. Now, even if we understand the second part of this, it would still be unclear why so general a claim ("the set of") must be believed in order to construe detritus as historical evidence. But there is also the more fundamental problem (which we now attend to) of there being in fact no clear prescription, owing to the ambiguity of the phrase "confirmed nomologicals." When Flew says that a law-candidate is "confirmed," does he mean merely that it is exceedingly probable relative to a body of inductive evidence which is large, wide-ranging, and thoroughly sought-out? Or does he mean that the law-candidate is exceedingly probable relative to *all* of our available and relevant information? If Flew means the *latter*, then it is uncontroversial that a critical historian should regard the set of "confirmed nomologicals" (in this wide sense of 'confirmed') currently available to the scientific community as being the best guide to what the (true) laws of nature are (whether or not his so regarding it is *necessary* for his construal of

detritus as historical evidence—(F5) would still be unmotivated). And let
us grant that we *in fact* have a corresponding and utterly uncontroversial
version of (F6). But the uncontroversial point above, and the uncontroversial version of (F6), are completely unhelpful to any Humean argument
against the credibility of the miraculous, since the (crucial) claim that a certain nomological which an alleged miracle would violate is "confirmed" in
this wide sense—that it is exceedingly probable relative to *all* of our available and relevant information, including the testimony to the miracle—
begs the question at issue. On the other hand, if when Flew speaks of a
law-candidate as being "confirmed" he means only the *former* description
above, then he has given us no reason whatever to believe that a critical
historian should regard the set of confirmed nomologicals (in this *narrow*
sense of 'confirmed') currently available to the scientific community as being in all cases the best guide to what the (true) laws of nature are, nor any
reason to believe the corresponding version of (F5), nor any good reason
to believe the corresponding version of (F6). Such claims as Flew's then
would again beg the question at issue. For why cannot, say, the solitary testimony to a miracle rightly persuade us that such-and-such a nomological
is simply *not true*, however "confirmed" in this narrow sense it may be? The
claim that such testimony cannot do this is simply the claim, (H), which
the Humean is supposed to be arguing for. There being no discernible
Flewian meaning for 'confirmed nomological' interestingly different from
both of the above, it seems that Flew must inevitably beg the question, either in his claims about the normative and exclusionary force of (in the
narrow sense) "confirmed nomologicals," or in his claim that such-and-
such nomologicals concerning which there is the attestation to a miracle
are in fact (in the wide sense) "confirmed." Where, then, is the "devastating objection" which Flew purports to find in Hume?

I end this chapter with a note about Flew's curious notion of "a conflict
between Science and History." I do not see how there can be the sort of
"unevenly matched" contest which Flew envisions; for science is based on
history. What, after all, are reports of experimental results but the detritus
of the past? If in order to construe detritus as historical evidence one must
already have in hand a generous supply of scientific conclusions, then (save
by some purely imaginary Renaissance Man of the laboratories) the game
could scarcely be played at all.

7

Hume's Argument as Reconstructed by Jordan Howard Sobel

§1

Why should anyone suppose that an apparent law of nature is probably true? Normally I think so myself, but that is when (as is usually the case) the apparent law is exceedingly probable, not only relative to the body of inductive evidence which so strongly supports it, but relative as well (or so it seems to me) to *all* of our available and relevant information, because no (seemingly) serious, capable, honorable, sober, sincere fellow has claimed to have observed a salient and gross empirical event which (if occurring) obviously would be a counterinstance to the apparent law (its status as a counterinstance depending on no assumptions about nonsalient or subtle empirical matters, such as the nonsalient state of laboratory equipment— we don't suppose that Moses or Saint Matthew went wrong because they mistook a green wire for a blue wire, or had not calibrated their instruments correctly, or were trying to detect some minute or ambiguous effect), *where also* the observation apparently was made carefully, thoroughly, and over a substantial period of time (as in attentively watching the slow parting of a sea, or in carefully attending to a man walking toward one on the sea—not as in a fleeting glance). I mention here such observational circumstances as *I would in fact require* for the credibility of testimony to a miracle. I am not here arguing, or even claiming, either that these should be required, or that they render the testimony credible—I am supposed to be told by the Humean why *even these* are unavailing. If the Humean were to say, "Let every man go his own way in such matters, without prejudice," I would readily agree. But this is not what the Humean says, or at least it is not what Hume says. Hume wishes to contrast those who are subject to "superstitious delusion," or who believe "ridiculous stories," with the "just reasoner," "reasonable people," "the wise and learned," and "men of sense." He speaks of "a miracle, supported by any human testimony," as being "more properly a subject of derision than of argument"; he speaks of "a cheat" and of "credulity and delusion," and claims that "no testimony for any kind of miracle has ever amounted to a probability."[1]

Where the apparent law is thus (as it seems to me) exceedingly probable relative to all that we know, I am happy to say (being a holist) that the apparent law is *exceedingly likely to be true*, simpliciter, and that there are "incredibly high odds against the occurrence of" a counterinstance to it.[2] But where there is the (even solitary) attestation to a miracle, and the above observational circumstances are met, I do *not* think that there are "incredibly high odds against" the occurrence of the miracle, or that the apparent law is even *probably* true. In such circumstances, I think that the miracle very probably occurred, and thus that the apparent law is very probably false. (Just as, in the urn analogy considered earlier, I would believe, indeed, that there is at least one red marble in the urn.) Now, what is the Humean argument for the claim that I am not to be counted among "reasonable people" or "men of sense"—that I am being somehow irrational? There seems to be no good argument at all for such a claim, or at least we have found none in Hume, or Mackie, or Mill, or Flew. Is there a *Bayesian* argument for the claim?

No, obviously there is not; just as it is obvious that there is no Bayesian argument for (H). What Bayesians say on the topic comes down (essentially) to this. If one is *already* persuaded that it is virtually certain that a particular kind of event never takes place, then one is properly persuaded by testimony which one *later* comes across which asserts the occurrence of an event of that kind (perhaps in the remote past) only if one is then persuaded that it is *even more certain* that such testimony is not false. But (even if this is so) the Bayesians perforce allow that if one is *first* persuaded (in Sunday school, for example) of the propitious parting of a sea, or that a crucified and spear-pierced dead man came back to vigorous life after two nights in a tomb, or that a few small loaves and fishes were multiplied at a man's will so as to feed several thousand hungry people, or that a man walked on the

---

[1] Hume, "Of Miracles," 110 ("superstitious"), 129 ("ridiculous"), 124 ("just"), 125 ("reasonable"), 126 ("wise"), 129 ("sense"), 124 ("derision"), 129 ("cheat"), 126 ("credulity"), 127 ("no testimony").

[2] Owen, 201.

surface of a warm sea, *before* one has acquired any inclination to suppose that "such things do not happen," then there is no *Bayesian* objection at all to continuing to believe (on the basis of even solitary testimony) that these events took place, at least if the early persuasion is permanent and permanently maximal—propositions describing the events as real occurrences having taken up permanent residence in one's "background knowledge," relative to which they ever have a probability equal to unity. Once the events are thus ensconced, no Bayesian argument will ever remove them, even after one learns that they are, in my sense, violations of apparent laws of nature. And so, obviously, there is no Bayesian argument for (H); for at least those who have been permanently maximally persuaded in childhood of the reality of what they (later) take to be miracles (in my sense)—or, say, those who read Moses *before* they read Lamb[3]—may be happy Bayesians, if Bayesians they wish to be.

But can they be happy Humeans? Does Hume not convict even these (perhaps *especially* these) of "superstitious delusion"? Does Hume not claim that "the *Christian Religion* not only was at first attended with miracles, but even at this day cannot be believed by any reasonable person without one . . . which subverts all the principles of his understanding"?[4] If so, we have still not the faintest argument for such a claim. Did ever a young Scotsman of the eighteenth century believe in the reality of the Christian miracles, and then not believe, that change was "founded on *Faith*, not on reason,"[5] so far as we have been able to ascertain.

What (had all gone well) would a Bayesian argument on this topic be able to establish? Let us look at the concluding paragraph of a paper by a rather careful Bayesian, Jordan Howard Sobel:

It was I suppose clear from the start *that*—though it may now be somewhat clearer *why*—if anyone were to tell you that a man had died and come back to life you had better not believe him. "The statement that a man has been raised from the dead would," Leslie Stephen wrote, "prove that its author was a liar,"—or at any rate, to temper the phrase on Stephen's behalf, the speaker of an untruth. More fully and precisely, it would prove this to anyone who, before news of the statement, thought the thing would be a miracle and a natural impossibility, and did not then think that the existence of

---

[3] Sir Horace Lamb, *Hydrodynamics* (Cambridge: Cambridge University Press, 1895).

[4] Hume, "Of Miracles," 131.

[5] Ibid., 130.

this testimony would, if it is false, be not only also a miracle and a natural impossibility, but an even *greater* miracle.[6]

Everything here seems to hinge on chronology. Now, I wonder how many people in our culture, before hearing the "good news" that Jesus "had died and come back to life," have already formed a belief that "the thing would be a miracle and a natural impossibility" in Sobel's sense of thinking that such an event (as we may put it) *almost certainly never happens* (that such events are, as Sobel says, "assigned positive infinitesimal probabilities").[7] The issue is not whether a child comes to Sunday school armed with a conscious notion of "infinitesimal probability" (which seems unlikely), but whether the child comes already having made (consciously or not) *any* such assignments, much less one specifically about the probability of human resurrections. In any event, there is obviously no Bayesian impediment to the uninterrupted belief of the child who first accepts the "good news" with childlike innocence; there is no *Bayesian* impediment, then *or thereafter*. But then, contrary to what Hume asserts, it is perfectly possible for a (Bayesian) "reasonable person" to believe the Christian religion without need of any epistemic "miracle" which "subverts all the principles of his understanding." One wonders, then, how well the Bayesians have captured what Hume meant to say.

This possible dependence on chronology will perhaps seem to the reader (as it certainly seems to me) to be rather strange. How can the rationality of believing in a miracle depend on, say, whether one has read Moses and Matthew first, and then Newton and Lamb, or Newton and Lamb first, and then Moses and Matthew? A notion of rationality according to which what one ought to conclude, having read so-and-so many books, might depend on the *order* in which they were read, is altogether alien to me.[8]

I should be much tempted, though, to say that the view of Hume as a "proto-Bayesian,"[9] or an "intuitive Bayesian,"[10] greatly illuminates the ba-

---

[6] Jordan Howard Sobel, "On the Evidence of Testimony for Miracles: A Bayesian Interpretation of David Hume's Analysis," *Philosophical Quarterly* 37 (1987): 186. (I have omitted the final sentence of Sobel's concluding paragraph.)

[7] Ibid., 175.

[8] In this connection see, however, Richard Jeffrey, "Alias Smith and Jones: The Testimony of the Senses," *Erkenntnis* 26 (1987): 391–399; reprinted in his *Probability and the Art of Judgment* (Cambridge: Cambridge University Press, 1992), 108–116.

[9] Owen, 199.

[10] Sobel, 181.

sis of his "general maxim": "no testimony is sufficient to establish a miracle, unless the testimony be of such a kind, that its falsehood would be
more miraculous, than the fact, which it endeavours to establish."[11] But
even if the Bayesian argument were not viciously circular (a matter which
we will come to in due course), and even waiving the worry about *order*
just mentioned, I am not convinced that the question of the capacity of
testimony to "establish a miracle" really has anything to do with, as John
Earman puts it, "the assignment of little numbers to propositions in accord
with the probability axioms."[12] *Establishing* seems to have to do with a notion of warrant (of that which added to true belief yields knowledge), a notion which there is perhaps, as Alvin Plantinga has argued, no plausible
Bayesian way of capturing.[13]

I should also be much tempted to say that the Bayesian analysis illuminates an otherwise obscure remark by Jesus, recorded in Saint Luke's Greek
as: *hos an mē dexētai tēn Basileian tou theou hōs paidion, ou mē eiselthē eis autēn*
("Whosoever shall not receive the kingdom of God as a little child shall in
no wise enter therein.").[14] But, of course, whenever one first hears of the
supposed Christian miracles (and after however much scientific training
and loss of innocence), there is no evident reason why one should not suppose that the falsehood of that testimony which exists in their favor would
be more improbable (and hence a "greater miracle") than the alleged miracles themselves. If there is any Humean argument to be given against such
a supposition, it is (admittedly, of course) not to be found in the writings
of the Bayesians.

§2

We turn now to the main difficulty for the "Bayesian Hume." I will present this objection as it applies to Sobel's elegant Bayesian reconstruction
of Hume's argument, but it will be evident that the point applies to other
Bayesian reconstructions across the board.

[11] Hume, "Of Miracles," 115–116. (I quote only part of Hume's stated maxim.)

[12] John Earman, *Bayes or Bust? A Critical Examination of Bayesian Confirmation Theory*
(Cambridge: MIT Press, 1992), 59.

[13] Alvin Plantinga, *Warrant: The Current Debate* (Oxford: Oxford University Press, 1993),
114–131.

[14] Luke, 18:17; King James translation; the Greek can be found in, e.g., Nestle-Aland,
Novum Testamentum Graece, 26th ed. (Stuttgart: Deutsche Bibelgesellschaft, 1979), 220.

Before we come to the main business, however, there are some preliminary matters to attend to. First, I want to note certain remarks made by Sobel. In a footnote, Sobel cites a paper by David Owen ("Hume, Miracles, and Prior Probabilities") which was "presented at the 28 th Annual Congress of the Canadian Philosophical Association, June 11, 1984." Sobel then adds: "I commented on his paper on that occasion."[15] I ask the reader to think about what one *learns* from these remarks by Sobel. (We will return to the matter later.)

Next, by way of beginning our brief excursion into Bayesian technicalities, we may contrast, as Plantinga has noted, "two quite different sorts of probabilities." Probabilities in the first group

are ordinarily established by statistical means, by broadly speaking empirical or scientific investigation. Further, these probabilities are *general*; what is probable is that a thing of one kind (a 19-year-old American male who smokes more than a pack a day) should also be a thing of another kind (a survivor to the age of 70), or that a member of one class (the class of two-year-old Rhode Island Reds from southern Wisconsin) should also be a member of another (the class of chickens that will contract coccidiosis within the next year). These probabilities may change over time (the probability that an American infant will reach the age of 50 is greater now than it was 100 years ago); and they do not depend upon what anyone knows or believes. Turning to the probabilities in the second group, note first that what is probable or improbable here is a *proposition*: Special Relativity, or The Linguistic Theory of the A Priori, or *there has been life on earth for more than 3 billion years*. Note second that these probabilities are explicitly or implicitly relative to some body of information or evidence; it is improbable, with respect to what we now know, that the earth is flat, but not with respect to what was known by a sixth-century Celt. Third, note that scientific or statistical investigation is not ordinarily relevant to the establishment of these probabilities, that is, to the probability of the proposition in question relative to the body of information in question (although of course such investigation is relevant to the establishment of that body of information). And finally, note that these probabilities contain an irreducibly *normative* element. It is epistemically extremely probable (given our circumstances) that the earth is round; hence, there is something wrong, mistaken, substandard in

---

[15] Sobel, 167 n. 5.

believing (in those circumstances) that it is flat; to believe this in our circumstances you would have to be a fool, or perverse, or dysfunctional, or motivated by an unduly strong desire to shock your friends.[16]

We will call probabilities like those of Plantinga's second group *epistemic* probabilities. It seems to be part of the common core of "Bayesianism" that epistemic probabilities are, or ought to be, person-relative "degrees of belief regimented according to the principles of the probability calculus."[17] I will follow here Earman's characterization of the matter:

Since propositions are the object of belief and since probability is being interpreted as degree of belief, probabilities will be assigned to objects that express propositions, namely sentences. More specifically, let S be a collection of sentences. The content and structure of S will vary from context to context, but at a minimum it is assumed that S is closed under finite truth-functional combinations. Then a *probability function* Pr is a map from S to $\mathbb{R}$ [the set of real numbers] satisfying at least the following restrictions:

$$Pr(A) \geq 0 \text{ for any } A \in S \tag{A1}$$

$$Pr(A) = 1 \text{ if } \vDash A \tag{A2}$$

$$Pr(A \vee B) = Pr(A) + Pr(B) \text{ if } \vDash \sim(A \,\&\, B) \tag{A3}$$

Here $\vDash A$ means that A is valid in the sense that A is true in all models or all possible worlds. ["Thus, if one wishes to be pedantic, a Bayesian probability space is a triple (W, S, Pr), where W is a set of possible worlds, S is a set of sentences or propositions, and Pr is a map from S to $\mathbb{R}$ satisfying the probability axioms."] . . . I assume at a minimum that S respects propositional logic. ["In particular, if A is a tautology, then $\vDash A$."] In this case (A1) to (A3) suffice to prove many of the familiar principles of probability, including the following:

$$Pr(\sim A) = 1 - Pr(A)$$

$$Pr(A) = Pr(B) \text{ if } \vDash A \leftrightarrow B$$

$$Pr(A \vee B) = Pr(A) + Pr(B) - Pr(A \,\&\, B)$$

$$Pr(A) \leq Pr(B) \text{ if } A \vDash B$$

[16] Plantinga, 115–116.
[17] Earman, 33.

Here $A \models B$ means that A semantically implies B in the sense that B is true in every model or possible world in which A is true.

Conditional probability may be introduced as a defined concept:

Definition   If $\Pr(B) \neq 0$, then $\Pr(A/B) \equiv \dfrac{\Pr(A \& B)}{\Pr(B)}$ [18]

Since

(B1) $\models B \leftrightarrow ((A \& B) \vee (\sim A \& B))$

we have

(B2) $\Pr(B) = \Pr((A \& B) \vee (\sim A \& B))$.

Since

(B3) $\models \sim((A \& B) \& (\sim A \& B))$

we have

(B4) $\Pr((A \& B) \vee (\sim A \& B)) = \Pr(A \& B) + \Pr(\sim A \& B)$.

Thus, by the definition of conditional probability, we have

(B5)   If $\Pr(B) \neq 0$, then $\Pr(A/B) = \dfrac{\Pr(A \& B)}{\Pr(A \& B) + \Pr(\sim A \& B)}$

Now, Sobel begins his Bayesian interpretation of Hume's argument by saying:

> My first and main proposal is that we take as a measure of "the evidence that would result for a positively probable piece of testimony", or, equivalently, of 'the credibility of a positively probable piece of testimony' the ratio of probabilities,
>
> $$\frac{\Pr[t(S) \ \& \ S]}{\Pr[t(S)]}$$
>
> wherein S *is a proposition affirming some state of affairs or fact* (for example, that the taxicab involved in the accident was blue), and t(S) *is a proposition affirming the existence of a piece of testimony to the effect that* S (for example, that the witness in the dock said that the taxicab involved in the accident was blue). The *numerator* above is the probability that the testimony *exists* (or will

exist)—that it has [been] (or will) be given—*and is true*. The *denominator* is the probability that it exists. And my claim, to repeat, is that the *ratio* measures the evidential potential relative to S of this possible [that is, "positively probable"] testimony. Since this ratio is by definition the conditional probability

$$Pr\ [S/t(S)]$$

my proposal is that 'the evidence of testimony' is measured by this conditional probability, that is, by the probability of its *truth* given its *existence*.[19]

Suppose that in fact S is a proposition (a sentence) affirming a miracle, and t(S) is a proposition affirming the existence of a piece of testimony "to the effect that S." Following Sobel's notation, let us use 'M' for 'S' and 't(M)' for 't(S)'. Then as an instance of (B5) we have (essentially) what Sobel calls "A Rule for the Evidence of Testimony for Miracles":[20]

$$(B6)\ If\ Pr[t(M)] \neq 0\ then\ Pr[M/t(M)] = \frac{Pr[M\ \&\ t(M)]}{Pr[M\ \&\ t(M)] + Pr[\sim M\ \&\ t(M)]}$$

The idea is that "the evidence of" the testimony whose existence t(M) affirms, for the miracle which M affirms, is (on the quite uncontroversial assumption that $Pr[t(M)] \neq 0$) to be "measured by" the conditional probability $Pr[M/t(M)]$, and thus by the expression at the far right of (B6). We come then to Sobel's main argument, which I quote at some length:

'Proofs', according to Hume, give rise to last degrees of assurance *in the absence of 'counter-proofs'*, but not always (Hume might have thought not ever) in the presence of 'counter-proofs', in which cases net *non*-extreme degrees of assurance can be produced. . . . For a quantitative gloss on Hume's concept of a miracle, we say that M asserts what would in a person's view be a miracle if and only if M is logically possible and there is what Hume would term a "proof" for this person against M. *And*, availing ourselves of the resources of a nonstandard probability theory, we say that there *is* a "proof" for a person against M if, for this person,

$$Pr(M) < i$$

for some positive infinitesimal i, and that such an inequality holds for a person if and only if there is, for this person, a "proof" against M and no

[19] Sobel, 167–168.
[20] Ibid., 173.

"proof" for M. . . . For the remainder of this section, we take 'M' to express what in a person's view would be a miracle, a miracle *for* which there
is *not* a "proof"—that is, M is to be an event against which there is a 'proof'
that is *not* opposed by a 'counter-proof', at least not yet. And we take 't(M)'
to express the existence of a piece of testimony for M such that for the person in question $Pr[t(M)] > 0$. By an application of the Rule for the Evidence of Testimony for Miracles, it follows from conditions imposed above
on probabilities of miracles that, for an infinitesimal that is less than or equal
to $Pr(M)$,

$$Pr[M/t(M)] = \frac{i}{i + Pr[\sim M \ \& \ t(M)]}.$$

There are two possibilities relevant to this ratio. Either $Pr[\sim M \ \& \ t(M)]$ is
not an infinitesimal, or it is one. If it is not an infinitesimal, then

$$Pr[M/t(M)] \simeq [\text{"is infinitely close to"}] \ 0,$$

and everything considered the testimony would lack "all" (more strictly,
"nearly all") credibility.

If $Pr[\sim M \ \& \ t(M)]$ *is* an infinitesimal, then the falsehood of the testimony—that it should exist though false, $[\sim M \ \& \ t(M)]$—would *itself* be a
miracle, and, supposing that $Pr[\sim M \ \& \ t(M)] = i'$,

$$Pr[M/t(M)] = \frac{i}{i + i'}.$$

Everything in *this* case would thus depend on which would be the greater
miracle: that the testimony should exist and be *true* so that $i' = Pr[\sim M \ \&$
$t(M)] > Pr[M \ \& \ t(M)] = i$; *or*, that the testimony should exist and be *false*,
so that $i = Pr[M \ \& \ t(M)] > Pr[\sim M \ \& \ t(M)] = i'$. If that the testimony
should exist and be *true*, then

$$Pr[M/t(M)] < .5.$$

If that the testimony should exist and be *false*, then

$$Pr[M/t(M)] > .5.$$

In this last case in which "the falsehood of testimony would be more miraculous," than would be its truth, and *only* in this case, can testimony for a
miracle "pretend to command . . . belief." . . . For presumably testimony
t(S) should engage belief only if $Pr[S/t(S)] > .5$.[21]

---

[21] Ibid., 174–177.

Now, why should testimony (whose existence t(M) affirms) for M be credible "for the person in question" only if for that person Pr[M/t(M)] > .5? *This* conditional probability Pr[M/t(M)] of which Sobel speaks is simply a function of the "prior probabilities" which appear on the right side of the equation in (B6), in the "Rule for the Evidence of Testimony for Miracles." There are two such "priors": Pr[M & t(M)] and Pr[~M & t(M)]. We recall that Plantinga noted (what no one would dispute) with regard to epistemic probabilities that "these probabilities are explicitly or implicitly relative to some body of information or evidence." Presumably Sobel is assuming that the above "priors" exist relative to "background knowledge" which does *not* include knowledge that t(M) holds. For otherwise Sobel obviously would be begging the question in supposing that "for the person in question" Pr(M), and hence Pr[M & t(M)], is an *infinitesimal*. Why should Pr[M & t(M)], or indeed Pr(M), be an infinitesimal relative to background knowledge which *includes* knowledge of the existence of the testimony in favor of the miracle? Simply to *assume* that t(M) does not constitute a "counter-proof" *for* M is obviously unhelpful; and if it *did* constitute for the person in question such a counter-proof then, as Sobel is well aware, there would be no reason to suppose that either Pr[M & t(M)] or Pr(M) is an infinitesimal. Obviously, then, when Sobel assumes that for the person in question Pr(M), and hence Pr[M & t(M)], is an infinitesimal, he is taking these probabilities to exist relative to background knowledge which does *not* include knowledge of the existence of the testimony in favor of the miracle.

This means that for the person in question the conditional probability Pr[M/t(M)] of which Sobel speaks exists also only as relative to that same background knowledge which does not include knowledge that t(M) holds. (It is not, in any *mathematical* sense, a "posterior" probability.) Why, then, should the value of this conditional probability be taken as a measure of the credibility of that testimony whose existence t(M) affirms *after* the person at issue learns of the existence of that testimony—as the person's posterior Pr(M)? Though Sobel is (curiously) silent about the matter, it is evident that he is tacitly assuming some sort of principle of Bayesian "conditionalization." (I will assume that the principle at issue is "classical" or "strict" conditionalization, as opposed to Jeffrey conditionalization, or some other such generalization of the classical idea.[22] It will be evident to

---

[22] On Jeffrey conditionalization, see Richard Jeffrey, *The Logic of Decision*, 2d ed. (New York: McGraw-Hill, 1983).

the reader, after our discussion, that Sobel cannot repair his case by appealing to one of these other principles.) Now, what is the principle of "strict conditionalization"? It is sometimes *misstated*. Plantinga, for example, describes it in the following way:

> We may put this requirement as follows: suppose C_0 is my credence function at a time t_0; and suppose I then learn (by observation, let's say) that B is true. What should C_1, my credence function at the next instant t_1, be? Since I have learned that B is true, $C_1(B) = 1$, of course, but what about the rest of what I believe? The idea is that I should now believe a proposition A to the degree to which A was probable on B according to my old credence function; I must conform to
>
> (Conditionalization) $C_1(A) = C_0(A/B) = C_0(A \& B)/C_0(B)$
> (where $C_0(B)$ is not zero).[23]

This is a *misstatement* of the principle because one can learn more than one thing at a time. For a correct statement of the principle, we may turn to Earman:

> The rule of *strict conditionalization* says that if it is learned for sure that E and if E is the strongest such proposition, then the probability functions Pr_{old} and Pr_{new}, representing respectively degrees of belief prior to and after acquisition of the new knowledge, are related by
>
> $$Pr_{new}(\cdot) = Pr_{old}(\cdot/E).[24]$$

Howson and Urbach describe the principle in the following terms: "if $P(h/e)$ is your conditional probability of h on e, and you learn e (but nothing stronger), then consequent upon this information, your degree of belief in h is, if you are consistent, equal to $P(h/e)$."[25] Note Earman's crucial qualification, "if E is the strongest such proposition," and Howson and Urbach's "but nothing stronger." Such a qualification is obviously necessary, since in learning E, I may at the same time also learn E & F. (At the same time, for example, I learn that the die came up prime and even, and that it came up prime. Pr_{old} (it came up 2/it came up prime) = .25. Pr_{old} (it came

[23] Plantinga, 122.
[24] Earman, 34.
[25] Colin Howson and Peter Urbach, *Scientific Reasoning: The Bayesian Approach* (La Salle, Ill.: Open Court, 1989), 258.

up 2/it came up prime and even) $= 1$. Obviously we do not want Pr_{new} (it came up 2) $= .25$, where "the new knowledge" is in fact not just that it came up prime but that it came up prime and even.)

This being understood, Sobel's argument collapses. For in the crucial *unstated* part of the argument—in the move from $Pr_{old}[M/t(M)] = x$ to $Pr_{new}(M) = x$, where it is "learned for sure" that $t(M)$ holds (which move is what taking the given conditional probability as "a measure" of the credibility of the testimony for the miracle comes to)—Sobel either begs the question or makes a wholly unjustified move. If he supposes that, quite in general, upon "receipt" (as Bayesians sometimes say) of knowledge of the existence of the testimony for the miracle one learns, or "learns for sure," that $t(M)$ holds *but nothing stronger*—in particular, *not also* that *the miracle occurred*—then he begs the question. Why suppose that in learning (or learning "for sure") that Moses *said* that the Sea of Reeds parted, I do not *also*, at the same time, learn (or learn "for sure") that the Sea of Reeds did in fact part? To insist that *learning* the former cannot also involve *learning* the latter is to beg the question. When we learn of the existence of the above-cited remark by Sobel that he commented on David Owen's paper in 1984, do we not at the same time learn that Sobel commented on David Owen's paper in 1984? (If not, when do we learn this?) If so, why should it be any different with Moses and a miracle? (The Humean, of course, *claims* that it is different, but argument for such a claim is what we have not yet found.) On the other hand, in the absence of such a general and question-begging insistence that learning $t(M)$ is never at the same time learning M, Sobel's implicit move from $Pr_{old}[M/t(M)] = x$ to $Pr_{new}(M) = x$ is wholly unjustified by any Bayesian principle which commends itself to the intellect.[26]

---

[26] For further objections (if any are needed) to the "Bayesianized Hume," see John Earman, "Bayes, Hume, and Miracles," *Faith and Philosophy* 10 (1993): 293–310.

[8]

Repetitions

The Beloved Disciple on high authority tells us that "God is light [*ho theos phōs estin*] and in him is no darkness at all."[1] The author of the letter "to the Hebrews" says that "our God is a consuming fire [*ho theos hēmōn pur katanaliskon*]."[2] Yet Hume tells us that nothing is afforded us in religion's "shadowy regions" but "the obscure, glimmering light."[3] Now, I own that the existence of God is not as obvious as the existence of the sun in the sky. God is at best an invisible and theoretical entity for most of us— we "have neither heard his voice at any time, nor seen his form [*eidos*]."[4] (We who have never seen God, and wonder why, perhaps have our explanation in the sixth beatitude.)

Most all of us, of course, believe in certain invisible entities (numbers and quarks, for example). We believe in them because some theory which best explains what we or others manifestly see and touch posits their existence. Rightly believing the theory, we believe in the invisible beings. Now, if seas are parted or walked on, or water turned to wine; if storms are stilled upon command and dead men rise; if "blind men see again, lame men walk, lepers are cleansed, and deaf men hear"—it may very well be (for all philosophy can say) that the best explanation of these extraordinary

---

[1] I John 1:5; King James translation; see Nestle-Aland, 615.
[2] Hebrews 12:29; King James translation; see Nestle-Aland, 585.
[3] Hume, *The Natural History of Religion*, in *Principal Writings on Religion including Dialogues concerning Natural Religion and* The Natural History of Religion, edited by J. C. A. Gaskin (Oxford: Oxford University Press, 1993), 172.
[4] John 5:37; mostly King James.

occurrences is a theological theory which (among other things) postulates the existence of "the God of Abraham, and of Isaac, and of Jacob." And neither Hume nor anyone else has given us any good philosophical reason why we ought not to accept (even on the testimony of *one* supposed witness) the occurrence of such miracles as the above, nor any good philosophical reason why, if indeed they happened, a certain theological theory might not be the best explanation of their occurrence. And such is the state of things.

Now, I have a certain fear: though no one will be able to produce a cogent Humean argument on this subject, the myth of its existence will persist among academicians, who are ever ready, especially in conversations with the pious, to call it from the vasty deep. So perhaps it will not hurt to belabor the obvious a bit, and look at a few more examples of explicitly or implicitly Humean arguments; though by now these must seem almost to refute themselves.

William L. Rowe, in his excellent *Philosophy of Religion*, states (without endorsing it) a version of Hume's argument:

The argument, simply put, proceeds as follows:

1. The evidence from experience in support of a law of nature is extremely strong.
2. A miracle is a violation of a law of nature.
   Therefore,
3. The evidence from experience against the occurrence of a miracle is extremely strong.[5]

The basic problem here is essentially the same one which we saw in our discussion of Mackie. If the first premiss means that "the evidence from experience" *in total*—including the testimony to the miracle—in support of the law of nature is "extremely strong," then the premiss begs the question. Why cannot the (even solitary) testimony to the miracle greatly evidentially outweigh the inductive or other evidence that supports the (apparent) law which the miracle would violate, making the overall experiential case for the law, say, very weak? (The Humean *says* that it cannot, but it is the justification for such a claim which is difficult to locate.) If on

---

[5] William L. Rowe, *Philosophy of Religion: An Introduction*, 2d ed. (Belmont, Calif.: Wadsworth, 1993), 121.

the other hand the first premiss means that "the evidence from experience"—*not* including the testimony to the miracle—in support of the law is extremely strong, then, even if this is so (there is a *sense* of it in which I agree it is so: the apparent law of nature is exceedingly probable relative to the inductive evidence that supports it), how is one to get from this to the desired Humean conclusion that the overall experiential case (which is the one we are interested in) against the occurrence of the miracle is "extremely strong" (i.e., that the occurrence of the miracle is exceedingly, or for that matter even slightly, improbable simpliciter)? We have discussed the difficulties in justifying such a move, with regard to Mackie's argument, and I will not repeat that discussion here, save to remind the reader that we are faced with what is formally a non sequitur. The Humean must at least acknowledge that there is here "a certain step taken; a process of thought, and an inference, which wants to be explained."[6]

Understand that I am not at all questioning the legitimacy of induction, if by 'induction' we mean the inference to 'All *A*s are *B*s' from the premiss 'All hitherto observed *A*s are *B*s' (*modulo* "projectibility," etc.). How could I be, since where the allegedly observed miracle was supposedly an *A* that was not a *B*, we do not even have, uncontroversially, the inductive premiss that 'All hitherto observed *A*s are *B*s'? I am questioning the legitimacy of the *forced move* from what is probable (or improbable) relative to partial evidence, to what is probable (or improbable) relative to total evidence.

Everyone questions this, to some extent. If, though a large and wide-ranging and thoroughly sought-out sample of *A*s are invariably *B*s, there is also globally wide and excellent testimony (as in Hume's example of the eight days of darkness) to the observation of *A*s that are not *B*s, no one would suppose that it is probable that all *A*s are *B*s, relative to all that we know. But whenever the available opposing testimony, to an *A* that is not a *B*, is that of *one* witness (of whatever apparent fine character and capacity and circumstance), it is *said* that we ought to think it probable that all *A*s are *B*s, relative to all that we know. *Why?* I am not (officially anyway) even denying this (much less asserting that we should always credit such testimony). I am asking for an explanation of the nature of that "decisive argument"[7] descending from Hume whose conclusion is (at least) that we should never credit such solitary testimony to a miracle.

---

[6] Hume, *An Enquiry concerning Human Understanding* (Selby-Bigge edition), 34.

[7] Hume, "Of Miracles," 110. Hume implies that Tillotson's "argument against the *real presence*" (transubstantiation) is "a decisive argument" and says, "I flatter myself, that I have

As I say, Rowe does not endorse the argument displayed above, and indeed he criticizes it; but his criticisms seem to me to be unnecessarily weak. He ends his critical discussion of the argument with two noteworthy sentences: First: "It remains true, however, that a reasonable person will require quite strong evidence before believing that [an apparent] law of nature has been violated."[8] The point, though, is that we have found no good reason to suppose that, even for "a reasonable person," the testimony of *one* supposed witness, of certain character and circumstance, to a miracle, may not constitute "quite strong evidence." Second: "It is easy to believe the person who claimed to see water run downhill, but quite difficult to believe that someone saw water run uphill."[9] It depends, it seems to me, on who says the latter, and in what circumstances, nor have philosophers found any objection to my viewing it this way. But if all that is meant is that some *psychological* difficulty attends believing the latter, then doubtless so.

The psychologist Nicholas Humphrey, in his lovely and interesting paean to skepticism, *Leaps of Faith: Science, Miracles, and the Search for Supernatural Consolation,* says the following:

> Hume's argument was based on probabilities. It stands to reason, he said, that when we have to decide between two rival hypotheses to explain something, to each of which we can assign an antecedent probability, we are obliged to accept the most probable as the best explanation.
>
> Suppose, for example (though not Hume's example), we know that someone has drawn a black ball from one or other of two bags, each of which contains a mixture of black and white balls. We do not know which bag the ball was drawn from. But we know that bag A contains at most 1 per cent black balls, while bag B contains at least 50 per cent. If we now have to say which bag we *think* the ball was drawn from, we can and must confidently say bag B.
>
> Now, if someone tells us they have witnessed an apparently paranormal phenomenon, the situation is similar. We know their testimony could have originated either from an objective fact about the world that was genuinely paranormal or from a propensity on the observer's part to make up a story. That is, it could have come, as it were, either from the 'Objective Fact bag',

---

discovered an argument of a like nature, which, if just, will, with the wise and learned, be an everlasting check to all kinds of superstitious delusion.".

[8] Rowe, 125.

[9] Ibid.

OF, or from the 'Human Invention bag', HI. In many cases we do not actually know which. We know however that the probability of finding a paranormal phenomenon in bag OF is very low indeed: otherwise the phenomenon would not be considered paranormal—indeed, years have gone by and the chances are that we ourselves have seldom if ever come across clear examples of paranormal phenomena in our own experience. We also know that the probability of finding such a phenomenon in bag HI is relatively high: otherwise human observers would have to be paragons of honesty and reliability, which we know they are not—indeed, every day of the week we have come across examples of people lying, exaggerating, misperceiving, misremembering, saying things for effect, and so on, and no doubt we have done it ourselves on some occasion. Hence, Hume argued, when we are required to choose one or other hypothesis about where the testimony has come from, we ought always to assume bag HI. . . . Hume's argument, so far as it goes, is perfectly solid. Given what we know about the world we live in, he must be right that the *balance of probability* is always going to be against evidence for the paranormal being what it seems to be.[10]

All that is obvious is that we are obliged to accept that explanation which is the most probable *simpliciter*—relative to *all* of our available and relevant information—as being the best explanation. The reason why, in the case of bags A and B, "we can and must confidently say" that the black ball came from bag B, is that—given the way the example is described—this hypothesis is uncontroversially the more probable relative to all of our available and relevant information. (It would be different if some trustworthy soul claims to have seen the ball removed from bag A.) What about the case of "bags" OF and HI? The phrase, "We know however that the probability of finding a paranormal phenomenon in bag OF is very low indeed," is (multiply) ambiguous, (in part) in a now familiar way. The probability is very low relative to what body of information? To information which *does* include some particular testimony to a paranormal phenomenon? Then the claim begs the very question at issue. To information which does *not* include this particular testimony to a paranormal phenomenon? Then how is the move made from this low probability to the desired low probability simpliciter? This is the move for which we as yet have found no justification.

It certainly will not do to say that "the probability of finding a para-

[10] Nicholas Humphrey, *Leaps of Faith: Science, Miracles, and the Search for Supernatural Consolation* (New York: Basic Books, 1996), 75–77.

normal phenomenon in bag OF" must be very low simpliciter, simply because "otherwise the phenomenon would not be considered paranormal."
(Recall Hume's "otherwise the event would not merit that appellation.")
There is nothing to be said against the definitional understanding of 'miracle' and 'paranormal phenomenon' (for me these are synonymous) which
we have here adopted, according to which an event is a miracle, or is a
paranormal phenomenon, in virtue of the fact that its occurrence would
contravene some apparent law of nature. Period. (Willed sea-partings, and
resurrections, presumably count under this head, as does the "raising of a
feather, when the wind wants ever so little of a force requisite for that purpose.") [11] It seems to me best to understand the terms in this way, and to
let the role of "the Deity, or . . . of some invisible agent" enter the picture
only as regards the explanation of these events, supposing we rightly believe such events to have occurred. First: Did someone rise from the dead?
Second: If so, what is the best explanation of this? (And why *cannot* a theological explanation turn out to be the best explanation of so extraordinary an event?) I believe that a certain miracle (in my sense of the word)
occurred: Jesus rose from the dead. In believing in this occurrence, and
that it was (in my sense) a miracle, I have neither inclination nor evident
obligation to add: "But probably it did not happen" (that is, "probably"
simpliciter it did not happen). On the contrary, I think it extremely probable, simpliciter, that this event took place (which is why I am a Christian).
Nor can any philosopher (or psychologist) convict me of an error here.
Obviously, Humphrey wants and needs to say that we know that the probability simpliciter of finding the Resurrection in bag OF "is very low indeed." But this in no evident way follows from the fact that the Resurrection is a miracle (or a paranormal phenomenon), in my sense. So what
is the argument for the claim? By all means, let it be "true by definition"
that, for any given *Humphrey-miracle* (or *Humphrey-paranormal* phenomenon), the probability simpliciter of its occurrence "is very low indeed." But
then what is the argument for the claim that the Resurrection (or such
other things as we are interested in) would have to have been a Humphrey-
miracle? (Maybe it is just like a Humphrey-miracle, save for the great probability simpliciter that it occurred.) And in the absence of such an argument, what *reason* do we have to suppose that the probability simpliciter of
the occurrence of the Resurrection (or of any such, in my sense, paranor-

---

[11] Hume, "Of Miracles," 115 n. 1.

mal phenomenon), of its being in bag OF, "is very low indeed"? No such reason is on the table.

Thus, we have been given no good reason to suppose that, in the relevant sense (of probability simpliciter), "the probability of finding a paranormal phenomenon [of finding one of *those things which are actually at issue*] in bag OF"—in either of the two possible senses of this: for a given paranormal phenomenon, the probability of finding *it* in bag OF; the probability of finding *some* paranormal phenomenon in bag OF—"is very low indeed." What about Humphrey's curious remark that "indeed, years have gone by and the chances are that we ourselves have seldom if ever come across clear examples of paranormal phenomena in our own experience"? Years have gone by and in *my own* experience I have never come across a clear example of a large ruby, but I accept on authority that such things exist. "But large rubies are not paranormal phenomena." So? Why there should be any rational difficulty in accepting on authority the existence of *paranormal* phenomena is what the Humean is supposed to be *explaining*. "But many people claim to have large rubies." But why there should be any rational difficulty in accepting even on *solitary* authority the existence of a paranormal phenomenon is also what the Humean is supposed to be explaining.

So for any given alleged paranormal phenomenon at issue, even if we allow that the probability simpliciter of finding it in bag HI is "relatively high," we have been given no good reason to suppose that the probability of finding it in bag OF cannot be higher still, unless it is supposed that the probability (of its being in bag HI) being "relatively high" necessitates that it is *higher than* the probability of its being in bag OF (and hence greater than .5, since obviously if one of these probabilities is n then the other is $1 - n$). (I am not really sure what Humphrey means here; "relatively high" *might* simply mean high in comparison to a *supposed* "very low" probability of finding the phenomenon in bag OF, in which case it *might* be that the probability of finding it in bag HI is less than .5—say, .49 being "relatively high" in comparison to .001—and hence also less than the real probability of finding it in bag OF!) So we are surely *obliged* to suppose the necessitation. But then the problem, of course, is that we in fact have been given no good reason to believe that, for a particular alleged paranormal phenomenon, the probability *simpliciter* of finding it in bag HI is (in the above required sense) "relatively high," this being the same matter we have already covered, now stated in different words. The probability simpliciter is the probability relative to *all* of our available and relevant information, including the testimony to the paranormal phenomenon. *Why* should we say that, relative to *this* information, the probability of "finding the paranormal phenomenon in bag HI"—the probability of its being a fiction rather than a fact—is "relatively high" rather than, say, extremely low? Isn't this the very issue on the table? That such a probability should be high rather than low all too obviously does not *follow* from the fact that not all human observers are "paragons of honesty and reliability" (I trust that Humphrey will allow that *some* are), nor even from the fact that *all* human observers are, as we may say, *fallible*. Fallibility had better not imply improbability of accuracy on any given particular point, lest history (and hence science) collapse. Why, then, should it imply improbability of accuracy on a *paranormal* point? "But the paranormal is so *unlikely*." And thus the Humean returns to the first square.[12]

The historian Bart D. Ehrman, in his recent book *The New Testament: A Historical Introduction to the Early Christian Writings*, gives the following Humean-sounding argument:

> As events that defy all probability . . . miracles . . . create an inescapable problem for historians. Since historians can only establish what probably happened in the past, and the chances of a miracle happening, by definition, are infinitesimally remote, they can never demonstrate that a miracle *probably* happened. . . . Even if there are otherwise good sources for a miraculous event, the very nature of the historical discipline prevents the historian from arguing for its probability.[13]

I leave the refutation of this bit of sophistry as an exercise for the reader. If the reader is not now well able to refute it, then my labors have been in vain.

The philosophical historian John Herman Randall, Jr., in his well-known *The Making of the Modern Mind*, rather breathlessly informs us:

---

[12] I should say that Humphrey himself says of Hume's argument that "cogent as it is, there are good reasons for not taking this argument to be the knock-down argument Hume meant it to be." But the caveat comes only to this: "We must recognise that an argument based on probabilities can never be more than that—a *probabilistic* argument. While it can provide a rule of thumb that tells us how the plausibility of one explanation compares with another, it surely cannot provide an absolute guarantee of where the truth lies" (77). Absolute guarantees, however, are not to the point.

[13] Bart D. Ehrman, *The New Testament: A Historical Introduction to the Early Christian Writings* (Oxford: Oxford University Press, 1997), 200.

It remained for Hume to administer the *coup de grace*. In his famous *Essay on Miracles* [*sic*], in 1748, he proved so conclusively that intelligent men have rarely questioned it since, that a miracle, in the sense of a supernatural event as a sign of the divinity of its worker, cannot possibly be established. Even could it be shown that the events recorded did actually take place, that they were supernatural, and that they suffice to establish a religion, it is impossible to demonstrate. No such event can contain any evidential value. . . . [F]or one who accepts Newtonian physics, unless he assumes that he has so complete a knowledge of the workings of nature as to be able to exclude every natural cause—a thing obviously impossible—it is impossible to prove that any given event was supernaturally produced. Whatever its cause, it is far easier to believe it effected by some natural factor. Hume's argument has never been refuted, and since it was fully understood no man has ever attempted to establish revelation upon any such purely external grounds.[14]

Though I am tempted to stop and explore what Randall might possibly mean by "easier," I will make no further comment save to refer the reader to our discussion of Mill above.

Martin Curd, in his review[15] of Joseph Houston's important book, *Reported Miracles: A Critique of Hume*,[16] chides Houston for giving "barely a mention" to a number of recent authors on our topic, among them J. C. A. Gaskin.[17] Lest I be chided myself on this particular, let us look at what Gaskin has to say. We are presented with the following "paraphrase of Hume's argument":

1. A weaker evidence can never destroy a stronger.
2. A wise man proportions his belief to the evidence.
3. Some things happen invariably in our experience, for example, that men die. In matters of fact these invariable experiences constitute certainties and are called, or form the basis of, laws of nature—"a firm and unalterable [unalterable because *past*] experience has established these laws."
4. Other things happen less than invariably in our experience, for example,

---

[14] John Herman Randall, Jr., *The Making of the Modern Mind: A Survey of the Intellectual Background of the Present Age* (Boston: Houghton Mifflin, 1926), 293–294. (This remains unchanged in the revised edition of 1940.)

[15] Martin Curd, review of *Reported Miracles: A Critique of Hume*, by Joseph Houston, *Mind* 106 (April 1997): 349–353.

[16] Joseph Houston, *Reported Miracles: A Critique of Hume* (Cambridge: Cambridge University Press, 1994).

[17] Curd, 353.

that one will survive a heart attack. In matters of fact these variable experiences constitute probabilities which admit of degrees ranging from strong (almost always happens) to weak (very seldom happens).

5. The veracity of human testimony is, from experience, normally a strong probability and as such amounts to a proof that what is reported took place. But sometimes the veracity of human testimony is a weak probability (as is always the case, according to Hume's arguments in Part 2, with reports of miracles). *Therefore*, from 3 and 4, when testimony is given which is contrary to our invariable experience, a probability, whether weak or strong, is opposing a certainty and (from 1 and 2) the wise man will believe the certainty.

6. But a miracle is "*a transgression of a law of nature* [see 3] *by a particular volition of the Deity.*" *Therefore*, "There must . . . be a uniform experience against every miraculous event, otherwise the event would not merit that appellation. And as a uniform experience amounts to a proof, there is here a direct and full *proof*, from the nature of the fact, against the existence of any miracle."[18]

The disentangling of the large tribe of ambiguities, question-begging assumptions, or non sequiturs, in the curious production displayed above, I leave mostly as an exercise for the reader. I will note that attention needs to be paid to the logical form of the various propositions. For example, it would be illuminating to be told to whom the mysterious word 'our' is supposed to apply. And if the claim is really that a "wise man" ought always to prefer even a parochial "certainty" to an authoritative "probability," why *exactly* is this so? (It will be hard to argue for this claim without running into a familiar non sequitur.) The truth of such a claim is hardly *obvious*. If earthquakes, or instances of Saint Elmo's fire, are "contrary to" Gaskin's *own* experience, ought he not to believe that they occur? (Note that photographs and films are a species of human testimony, as is evident from reflection on photographs of "flying saucers" and documentary footage of "alien autopsies.") If experience not my own counts as part of "our experience," then *whose*, and *why*, and why not the miracle-reporter's (in which case there would be no "certainty" opposed to the miracle). Suppose you say: "Experiences strange to me reported by *many* are more often true than experiences strange to me reported by only *one*." And you

---

[18] J. C. A. Gaskin, "Hume on Religion," in *Cambridge Companion to Hume*, ed. Norton, 329–330.

learned that from history books or newspapers, I suppose; from believing things you have been told.

Certain remarks by Gaskin elsewhere[19] suggest that Gaskin, or Gaskin's Hume, may want to say the following. The testimonial evidence in favor of the existence of, say, earthquakes is strong (as I agree it is) whereas that in favor of, say, the reality of the Resurrection is "weak," and where such evidence is "weak" it is rightfully overridden (for the wise man) by "the improbability of the event, when measured by our [purely the wise man's own, I surmise] normal experience."[20] But then *on what grounds* would one say that (even solitary) testimony such as we actually have to the reality of the Resurrection is "weak" evidence?

Gaskin refers above to "Hume's arguments in Part 2" as purporting to establish such a point, but it will not suffice merely to propose, for example, "a list of tough-minded requirements for such evidence"[21] (as in the second paragraph of the second part of Hume's essay) concerning the "sufficient number" of the witnesses, their requisite "unquestioned good-sense, education, and learning," their requisite "undoubted integrity," their requisite "credit and reputation in the eyes of mankind," and the "public manner . . . in [a] celebrated . . . part of the world" in which the attested events are required to have been performed,[22] and then to assert without argument that because these or other hazily specified "requirements" are not satisfied the testimonial evidence in favor of the Resurrection is weak. (In Hume, for example, we find only the bare assertion that such "circumstances are requisite to give us a full assurance in the testimony of men.")[23] *How many* witnesses to a miracle are necessary, *and why*? How "unquestioned" must their good sense, education, and learning be, and why? (Hume says that it must be "such . . . as to secure us against all delusion in themselves,"[24] but what is needed for *that*, and why? Would, for example, expertise in Jewish law be sufficient?) How "undoubted" must their integrity be, and why? (Hume says that it must be "such . . . as

---

[19] J. C. A. Gaskin, *Hume's Philosophy of Religion*, 2d ed. (New York: Macmillan, 1988), 135–165. See especially 151–159. (Note the discussion of the "Indian Prince Argument" on 151–152, and of the issue of "weak evidence" on 154–159.)

[20] Ibid., 155.

[21] Ibid., 156.

[22] Hume, "Of Miracles," 116.

[23] Ibid., 117.

[24] Ibid., 116.

to place them beyond all suspicion of any design to deceive others,"[25] but what is needed for *that*, and why? Is canonization perhaps sufficient?) How great a "credit and reputation in the eyes of mankind" must they have had, and why? (Hume says that it must be such that they would have had "a great deal to lose in case of their being detected in any falsehood,"[26] but— aside from the fact that one's life is a great deal to lose—why exactly cannot humble folk be credible witnesses to miracles?) How *public* must the miracle be, how *celebrated* the locale, and why? (Hume says that it must be so "as to render the detection [of any falsehood] unavoidable,"[27] but— aside from the fact that such detection is never in principle literally "unavoidable" [witness conspiracy theories, and the like]—we are left rather in the dark as to what degrees of publicity and celebrity are rightly required in order to render such detection sufficiently likely. Would eleven or more witnesses, or perhaps five hundred, in a then-famous city hostile to the miracle report be sufficient? If not, why not?)

Nor will it do simply to assert without argument that the mere "possibility of enthusiastic self-deception"[28] (owing to the "passion of *surprise and wonder*")[29] undermines the testimony to the miraculous. Perhaps (for all Hume gives us any good reason to believe) in the case at least of the more weighty and realistically reported miracles the love of wonder is quite sufficiently counterbalanced by the love of order,[30] and when the greatest matters are at stake men become the most sober.[31] The report of a re-vivified well-known public figure who is claimed to be Messiah, Son of God, and Emmanuel may have been far more sobering to a devout Jew than "miraculous accounts . . . of sea and land monsters."[32] Hume has not shown us otherwise, his remark that "if the spirit of religion join itself to the love of wonder, there is an end of common sense"[33] being the barest of assertions. Nor, of course, has he given us the least reason to agree that

[25] Ibid.

[26] Ibid.

[27] Ibid., 116–117.

[28] Gaskin, *Hume's Philosophy of Religion*, 157.

[29] Hume, "Of Miracles," 117.

[30] Cf. Keith E. Yandell, *Hume's "Inexplicable Mystery": His Views on Religion* (Philadelphia: Temple University Press, 1990), 332.

[31] Cf. Houston, *Reported Miracles*, 151–152.

[32] Hume, "Of Miracles," 117.

[33] Ibid.

there are "many instances of forged miracles"[34] of the same and relevant character. Even if mankind had a "strong propensity . . . to the extraordinary and the marvellous,"[35] this would be quite unhelpful to the Humean, in lieu of an *argument* that such a propensity is *unrestrained*, and would not be overruled by sobriety and the love of order (and, say, fear of punishment, terrestrial or divine) in the case at hand. (I shall only note, but not comment upon, the curious fact that although Hume says that "a suspicion against" reports of the extraordinary and the marvelous "is our natural way of thinking, *even* with regard to the most common and most credible events" [my emphasis], he supposes that in regard to matters of great importance this "natural way of thinking" will somehow be lacking in "the generality of mankind," reserved alone for the "man of sense.")[36]

Nor, of course, will it do simply to assert without argument that because, allegedly, "miraculous relations . . . are observed chiefly to abound among ignorant and barbarous nations"[37] such reports are not to be believed. We are given no reason to suppose that even "ignorant and barbarous" Jews would not have known the difference between a corpse and a dinner guest, or that they would have been any less skilled in establishing the reality of a dinner guest than were the wise and civilized Gentiles of Athens or Rome.

Hume's "*fourth* reason, which diminishes the authority of prodigies," is "that there is no testimony for any . . . that is not opposed by an infinite number of witnesses" to supposed miracles in support of "contrary" religions.[38] This objection might seem to presuppose that (among other things) evidence *for* a theory—evidence which magnifies the theory's probability of being true—must at the same time be evidence *against* any *incompatible* theory; that it must magnify the probability of the incompatible theory's being *false*. Hume says that

> in matters of religion, whatever is different is contrary; and . . . it is impossible the religions of ancient Rome, of Turkey, of Siam, and of China should, all of them, be established on any solid foundation. Every miracle, therefore, pretended to have been wrought in any of these religions (and all

[34] Ibid., 118.
[35] Ibid.
[36] Ibid., 118–119.
[37] Ibid., 119.
[38] Ibid., 121. Talk of the "infinite" here is, of course, hyperbole.

of them abound in miracles), as its direct scope is to establish the particular system to which it is attributed; so has it the same force, though more indirectly, to overthrow every other system.[39]

But the claim mentioned above (if indeed Hume is presupposing it) is patently false. In a random lottery with a thousand tickets labeled from '1' to '1000', evidence which consists in our learning that the winning number is greater than 200 but less than 211 (where we learn nothing else of significance about the matter) makes it one hundred times more likely than it was that the winning number is 209; but it *also* makes it one hundred times more likely than it was that the winning number is 207, which is an incompatible theory. Both theories have their probabilities magnified by this evidence. And why may we not allow that *every* miracle report magnifies the probability of its intended supernatural theory ("the particular system to which it is attributed"), or even that *all* miracle reports magnify the probabilities of *all* supernatural theories, albeit to different degrees? Hume, at least, has given us no good reason to suppose otherwise. The claims, for example, that such evidence as we actually have that the Buddha flew *magnifies* the probability that Buddhism (in some or all of its variants) is true, or that the rather ambiguous miracle reports cited by Hume from Tacitus and Suetonius[40] either individually or jointly magnify the probability that Serapisism is true, may very well be (and quite rightly so, in my opinion) utterly uncontroversial. But such claims are quite congenial to the Christian, and of no service to the Humean, in light of the failure of the above-mentioned principle.

Of course, in the above example about the lottery, 207 and 209 are still each *unlikely* (relative to the evidence specified) to be the winning number, each now having one chance in ten. And, noting Hume's phrase above, "established on [a] solid foundation," perhaps we should say that the principle at issue is *something* along the lines of: evidence relative to which a theory is *probably true* must at the same time be evidence relative to which any incompatible theory is *probably false*. If in regard to the above lottery we learn that the winning number is greater than 200 but less than 204 (and we learn nothing else of significance about the matter) this evidence is, un-

[39] Ibid.
[40] Ibid., 122. The references are to Cornelius Tacitus, *Historiae*, book IV, chap. 81, and to Gaius Suetonius Tranquillus, *De Vita Caesarum*, book VIII, the first part ("Divus Vespasianus"), the seventh chapter of that part.

controversially, evidence relative to which it is probably true that the winning number is odd, and evidence relative to which it is probably false that the winning number is even. Or perhaps (or, even, probably, though for reasons we will not go into) Hume has in mind something along the lines of: evidence relative to which a theory is *certainly* true (*entailing* evidence) must at the same time be evidence relative to which any incompatible theory is *certainly* false. Fine, perhaps so; what then? How would any such principles be helpful to the Humean in the case at hand? And what argument would there be that the Christian is obliged to suppose that such evidence as we actually have that the Buddha flew is evidence relative to which Buddhism is probably true (much less, certainly true), or that the miracle reports of Tacitus and Suetonius either individually or jointly constitute evidence relative to which Serapisism is probably true?

With regard to the report by Tacitus, Hume says the following:

> One of the best attested miracles in all profane history, is that which Tacitus reports of Vespasian, who cured a blind man in Alexandria, by means of his spittle, and a lame man by the mere touch of his foot; in obedience to a vision of the god Serapis, who had enjoined them to have recourse to the Emperor, for these miraculous cures. The story may be seen in that fine historian; where every circumstance seems to add weight to the testimony, and might be displayed at large with all the force of argument and eloquence, if any one were now concerned to enforce the evidence of that exploded and idolatrous superstition. The gravity, solidity, age, and probity of so great an emperor, who, through the whole course of his life, conversed in a familiar manner with his friends and courtiers, and never affected those extraordinary airs of divinity assumed by Alexander and Demetrius. The historian, a cotemporary writer, noted for candour and veracity, and withal, the greatest and most penetrating genius, perhaps, of all antiquity; and so free from any tendency to credulity, that he even lies under the contrary imputation, of atheism and profaneness: The persons, from whose authority he related the miracle, of established character for judgement and veracity, as we may well presume; eye-witnesses of the fact, and confirming their testimony, after the Flavian family was despoiled of the empire, and could no longer give any reward, as the price of a lie. *Utrumque, qui interfuere, nunc quoque memorant, postquam nullum mendacio pretium.* To which if we add the public nature of the facts, as related, it will appear, that no evidence can well be supposed stronger for so gross and so palpable a falsehood.[41]

<hr />

[41] Hume, "Of Miracles," 122–123. In a footnote to this passage, Hume says that "Suetonius gives nearly the same account *in vita* Vesp." I note that Hume conflates the two ac-

I take it that Hume is here suggesting that the account given by Tacitus is *at least* as fine historical evidence in favor of its miraculous events, as that given in the New Testament is in favor of the Resurrection, and that Hume has in mind some argument roughly of the following sort:

Given the relative excellence of the evidence from Tacitus, the Christian ought to agree that:

(S1) The evidence in favor of the Resurrection is evidence relative to which Christianity is probably true, *only if* the report by Tacitus is evidence relative to which Serapisism is probably true.

But, given that

(S2) Christianity and Serapisism are incompatible and given the above-mentioned principle about probable truth:
(S3) Evidence relative to which a theory T is probably true must at the same time be evidence relative to which any theory T' incompatible with T is probably false

the Christian ought to agree that

(S4) The evidence in favor of the Resurrection is evidence relative to which Christianity is probably true, *only if* the report by Tacitus is evidence relative to which Christianity is probably false.

But then, since (again) the account given by Tacitus is at least as fine historical evidence in favor of its miraculous events, as that given in the New Testament is in favor of the Resurrection, the Christian ought to agree [so the argument goes] that he has at least as good evidence that Christianity is probably *false*, as he has that Christianity is probably true. So he ought not to believe that Christianity is true, or at least he ought not to do so *on the basis* of the available historical evidence.

There would be a variety of difficulties in trying to convert the above rough sketch into a formally valid argument with seemingly compelling

---

counts—it is only Suetonius who speaks of a man who is lame (*debili crure*); in the account by Tacitus, that man has a "diseased hand" (*manum aeger*). (This seems a curious error on Hume's part, ironic in its context.) The Latin sentence which Hume quotes from Tacitus is the final sentence from the chapter cited above in note 40; see its translation by Moore below.

premisses, but our time will be most profitably spent in focusing simply on
the main point at issue, which is whether the (well-informed) Christian is
at all obliged to suppose that the account given by Tacitus is at least as fine
historical evidence in favor of its miraculous events, as that given in the
New Testament is in favor of the Resurrection. Here there is nothing to
do but to look in detail at the account given by Tacitus. (I will assume that
the reader is familiar with the evidence in favor of the Resurrection.) Here
(more or less) [42] is what Tacitus actually wrote:

> Per eos mensis quibus Vespasianus Alexandriae statos aestivis flatibus dies et
> certa maris opperiebatur, multa miracula evenere, quis caelestis favor et
> quaedam in Vespasianum inclinatio numinum ostenderetur. E plebe Alexan-
> drina quidam oculorum tabe notus genua eius advolvitur, remedium caeci-
> tatis exposcens gemitu, monitu Serapidis dei, quem dedita superstitionibus
> gens ante alios colit; precabaturque principem ut genas et oculorum orbis
> dignaretur respergere oris excremento. Alius manum aeger eodem deo auc-
> tore ut pede ac vestigio Caesaris calcaretur orabat. Vespasianus primo inri-
> dere, aspernari; atque illis instantibus modo famam vanitatis metuere, modo
> obsecratione ipsorum et vocibus adulantium in spem induci: postremo aes-
> timari a medicis iubet an talis caecitas ac debilitas ope humana superabiles
> forent. Medici varie disserere: huic non exesam vim luminis et redituram si
> pellerentur obstantia; illi elapsos in pravum artus, si salubris vis adhibeatur,
> posse integrari. Id fortasse cordi deis et divino ministerio principem elec-
> tum; denique patrati remedii gloriam penes Caesarem, inriti ludibrium
> penes miseros fore. Igitur Vespasianus cuncta fortunae suae patere ratus nec
> quicquam ultra incredibile, laeto ipse vultu, erecta quae adstabat multitu-
> dine, iussa exequitur. Statim conversa ad usum manus, ac caeco reluxit dies.
> Utrumque qui interfuere nunc quoque memorant, postquam nullum men-
> dacio pretium. [43]

Here is the translation of the above given by Clifford H. Moore:

> During the months while Vespasian was waiting at Alexandria for the reg-
> ular season of the summer winds and a settled sea, many marvels [*multa mira-
> cula*] occurred to mark the favour of heaven and a certain partiality of the

---

[42] Abstaining on issues of punctuation and capitalization, and other such minor textual
matters.

[43] Tacitus, Loeb Classical Library (Cambridge: Harvard University Press, 1931), vol. 2,
158–160. Henceforth "*Loeb.*" Aside from certain matters of capitalization, this text is identical to that given in Tacitus, *Historiarum Libri*, ed. C. D. Fisher (Oxford: Clarendon Press,
1911), 224–225.

gods toward him. One of the common people of Alexandria, well known
for his loss of sight [*oculorum tabe notus*], threw himself before Vespasian's
knees, praying him with groans to cure his blindness, being so directed by
the god Serapis [*monitu Serapidis dei*], whom this most superstitious of nations worships before all others; and he besought the emperor to deign to
moisten his cheeks[44] and eyes with his spittle [*oris excremento*]. Another,
whose hand was useless [*manum aeger*], prompted by the same god [*eodem deo
auctore*], begged Caesar to step and trample on it [*ut pede ac vestigio Caesaris
calcaretur . . .*]. Vespasian at first ridiculed these appeals and treated them with
scorn; then, when the men persisted, he began at one moment to fear the
discredit of failure, at another to be inspired with hopes of success by the appeals of the suppliants and the flattery of his courtiers: finally, he directed the
physicians to give their opinion as to whether such blindness and infirmity
[*caecitas ac debilitas*] could be overcome by human aid [*ope humana superabiles
forent*]. Their reply treated the two cases differently: they said that in the first
the power of sight had not been completely eaten away [*non exesam vim luminis*] and it would return if the obstacles were removed [*et redituram si
pellerentur obstantia*]; in the other [*illi*], the joints [which] had slipped and become displaced [*elapsos in pravum artūs*] . . . could be restored [*posse integrari*]
if a healing pressure [*vis:* force] were applied to them [*si salubris vis adhibea-
tur*].[45] Such perhaps was the wish of the gods, and it might be that the emperor had been chosen for this divine service; in any case, if a cure were obtained, the glory would be Caesar's, but in the event of failure, ridicule
would fall only on the poor suppliants. So Vespasian, believing that his good
fortune was capable of anything and that nothing was any longer incredible,
with a smiling countenance, and amid intense excitement on the part of the
bystanders, did as he was asked to do. The hand was instantly restored to use
[*statim conversa ad usum manus*], and the day again shone for the blind man [*ac
caeco reluxit dies*]. Both facts are told by eye-witnesses even now when falsehood brings no reward.[46]

Note what the *medici* say. The "blind" man, the man well known for his
loss of sight (*oculorum tabe notus*), perhaps was not altogether physically

---

[44] Or, perhaps, his *eyelids*; as in the early Latin poet Quintus Ennius's apparent use of
'*genas*'. See *Remains of Old Latin*, vol. 1, edited and translated by E. H. Warmington (Cambridge: Harvard University Press, Loeb Classical Library, 1935), 178–179.

[45] The masculine fourth-declension noun "*artus*" here is the plural accusative *artūs* (and
so in the context means "the joints"), being thus in agreement with the masculine plural
accusative perfect passive participle "*elapsos*" (*ēlapsōs*, from *ēlābor*) in the participial clause.
(I surmise that the report of the physicians is indirect discourse, and that "*vim*" and "*artus*"
are Subject Accusatives. Thus the plural *artūs*; so again "the joints.")

[46] Clifford H. Moore, *Loeb*, 159–161.

blind, since "the power of sight had not been completely eaten away" (*non exesam vim luminis*) and will return if the "obstacles" be driven away, whatever exactly that may mean. This description seems to be, as Antony Flew has suggested, at least compatible with its being the case that the man was suffering from a merely psychosomatic blindness.[47] How, then, are we to assess the significance of the somewhat vague claim that "the day again shone for the blind man" (*caeco reluxit dies*)?

As for the man with a "diseased hand" (*manum aeger*), the description which Tacitus has the physicians give ("*elapsos in pravum artus*") is at least compatible with its being the case that the man had a mere *dislocation* ("the joints [which] had slipped and become displaced"), cured by the "tread" of Vespasian's foot. That, indeed, the description is to be *read* as referring to a dislocation, seems to be a view widely shared by scholars. Not only does Moore (above) take it that way, but so too, for example, does Bassols de Climent in his commentary on the *Historiae*,[48] and so too do Gerber and Greef in their *Lexicon Taciteum*.[49] Thus also is it understood in the *Oxford Latin Dictionary*.[50] I should note, though, that some scholars read the description as speaking of a less specific sort of infirmity. Church and Brodribb, for example, construe it as speaking of a hand "which had fallen into a diseased condition."[51] Cartlidge and Dungan construe it as speaking of the joints which "had fallen into deformity."[52] (Of course, a dislocation is one *kind* of "diseased condition" and "deformity.") In any event, given that the description is, uncontroversially, *at least* compatible with its being the case that a mere dislocation was at issue, the fact that the "tread"[53] of Vespasian's foot resulted in the hand's being "instantly restored to its use" is somewhat equivocal evidence of a miracle.

[47] See Flew's introduction to Hume, *Of Miracles*, 15.

[48] Cornelio Tácito, *Historias*, Libro Cuarto, edited and with a commentary by M. Bassols de Climent (Madrid-Barcelona, 1955), 141.

[49] A. Gerber and A. Greef with C. John, *Lexicon Taciteum*, 16th ed. (Leipzig: B. G. Teubner, 1903). See the relevant remark in the entry for *elabor*, 342.

[50] *Oxford Latin Dictionary*, edited by P. G. W. Glare (Oxford: Clarendon Press, 1982). See the relevant remarks in the entry for *elabor*, 596.

[51] *The Complete Works of Tacitus*, translated by Alfred John Church and William Jackson Brodribb, edited by Moses Hadas (New York: Random House, Modern Library, 1942), 652.

[52] David R. Cartlidge and David L. Dungan, eds., *Documents for the Study of the Gospels*, rev. ed. (Minneapolis: Fortress Press, 1994), 155.

[53] Contrary to what Hume implies in his errant summary of Tacitus, there is nothing in the Latin which obliges us to construe Tacitus as reporting that it was but (as Hume says) "the mere touch" of Vespasian's foot which effected the cure.

Suppose, then, that a Christian were to say that such evidence of miraculous occurrences pales in comparison to that given in favor of the Resurrection, which latter evidence involves reports, either written by eyewitnesses or earnestly conveyed by them to their acquaintances, of very salient and collectively observed appearances (involving talking, touching, and eating) made by a man who was formerly and quite uncontroversially *dead*.[54] What historical error, exactly, would the Christian be making? Hume, at least, does not tell us; and so it has scarcely been established by Hume that the (well-informed) Christian is obliged to suppose that the account given by Tacitus is at least as fine historical evidence in favor of its miraculous events, as that given in the New Testament is in favor of the Resurrection.

Perhaps, though, Hume's point, in his "*fourth* reason, which diminishes the authority of prodigies," is simply that there are *so many* miracle reports, variably in support of *so many* religions incompatible with Christianity, that—though perhaps none of these reports or subgroups of reports is evidence relative to which its intended religion is probably true—*collectively* they must be evidence relative to which it is probably the case that some religion incompatible with Christianity is true, and evidence relative to which Christianity is probably false; just as in a game with a thousand equal chances of winning, the player who has three hundred chances will probably lose, though his (say) hundred competitors have but seven chances each.

There are a variety of problems with such a Humean suggestion, but the most salient one is that Hume then would need an argument, which he does not give, for the denial that Christianity may turn out actually to have, as it were, *six hundred* chances, and its hundred competitors but four chances each. Who knows but that the evidence in favor of the Resurrection might turn out on historical grounds to be vastly stronger—in terms,

---

[54] For an introduction to the compelling reasons for supposing that Jesus *died* on the cross, see (in addition to the account in the New Testament itself) William D. Edwards et al., "On the Physical Death of Jesus Christ," *Journal of the American Medical Association* 255 (March 21, 1986): 1455–1463, and the interview with Alexander Metherell, M.D., in Lee Strobel, *The Case for Christ: A Journalist's Personal Investigation of the Evidence for Jesus* (Grand Rapids, Mich.: Zondervan, 1998), 191–204. For an introduction to the historical evidences pertaining to the nature of crucifixion, see Martin Hengel, *Crucifixion in the Ancient World and the Folly of the Message of the Cross* (Philadelphia: Fortress Press, 1977). (Perhaps I should note that the title contains an allusion to I Corinthians 1:18; the word of the cross is "folly" [*mōria*] *tois apollumenois*, "to the perishing.")

for example, of our knowledge of *who* the alleged witnesses were, and of their spatiotemporal well-suitedness to have observed *distinctly* the *salient* occurrences at issue—than that, than even the totality of that, evidence in favor of miracles alleged in support of religions genuinely in competition with Christianity? After all, *who* exactly claims to have seen the Buddha walk in the sky, to have witnessed flame from him on high? When ever did Shiva serve breakfast on the seashore, or let his hand be touched by ten or more? Who ever clearly heard, or spied, Thor the thunderer, or gazed on somber one-eyed Odin? Who claims in olden time to have *spoken* with Osiris-who-died, again alive, Isis-revived? Who makes the claim—and on what basis—to a visitation from Serapis, the very god (no dainty in a dream)? What ever even seemed to be radiant Apollo or the lithe-limbed Huntress, to be foundrous Poseidon or lively Aphrodite? Whose eye has seen the *Nymphae*, or the *Musae*, or Zeus in the golden rain?

In short, the "arguments" of the second part of Hume's essay need detain us no further.

Suppose, however, that Hume (or Gaskin) is content to apply, without suitable argument, the epithet 'weak' to the testimonial evidence pertaining to the Resurrection, or perhaps, simply to say: "This is just what I mean by 'weak evidence'." Why then, freely allowing them whatever *notion* of "weak evidence" they may wish to have (it will not be my notion), and even allowing that in that sense the testimonial evidence in favor of the Resurrection is "weak," we must then ask why evidence which is in *that* sense "weak" *ought* to be overridden (even for the wise) by "the improbability of the event, when measured by our normal experience." On this central *normative* matter, Gaskin is (in the end, as we shall see), and Hume *in effect* is, completely silent. If either Gaskin or Hume had anything to say here, it perforce would be that elusive cogent Humean argument for (H), or for something like (H), from the *first* part of Hume's essay, which we have been seeking and which seems not to exist. (This is one reason why the argument of the first part of Hume's essay must ever be, as Mackie says, the "main argument.") In the presence of this epistemological silence, nothing at all is to be gained by a tendentious application of the word 'weak'.

To return to our earlier discussion, it is of course not yet clear to what extent Gaskin *endorses* the "argument" in the "paraphrase of Hume's argument" displayed above. In *Hume's Philosophy of Religion* Gaskin says, unhelpfully, that "it is decisive when applied to weak evidence but indecisive when applied to evidence which would be regarded as conclusive apart from the improbability of what is reported." [55] (Aside from a certain mystery about what it is to "apply" an argument, this is *unhelpful* because we have as yet been given no principled guidance as to what is *justly* called "weak," or "conclusive," or to the *significance* of evidence being "weak" in a tendentiously stipulative sense of that word.) In "Hume on Religion" Gaskin says, rightly enough, that the "above argument has provoked many questions," of which he lists six, the sixth being: "With what justification can we use the exceptional nature of an event as grounds for rejecting testimony that the alleged event took place?" [56] Gaskin rightly says that it is "this final question which is crucial in assessing and understanding Hume's . . . argument." He then makes the following mysterious remarks:

> The position I would defend with regard to question (vi) is this: Hume's argument is an accurate formal representation of the norm of rationality we all in fact apply, or try to apply, in our search for historical truth. Furthermore, when applied to the reports to which Hume has to apply it in order to damage the credentials of the Christian revelation—namely, to the biblical reports of miracles in general and to the Resurrection in particular—the norm is successful in showing that these reports would be rejected for the reasons he gives, if they occurred in contexts in which religious faith was not involved. [57]

What Gaskin means by speaking of an *argument* as being "an accurate formal representation" of a *norm* entirely escapes me, but I suppose that the "norm of rationality" at issue here is something along the lines of, "Don't believe testimony to an alleged event when that alleged event 'conflicts with all our experience as codified in the laws of nature'" [58] (the "all our experience" presumably not including the alleged event). If something like this is the norm at issue, then what is Gaskin's point? He says that "we all in fact apply, or try to apply" it in "our search for historical truth." As a sociological generalization, this is simply false; I am myself a counter-example. Perhaps Gaskin means that "we all in fact apply, or try to apply" the norm in our search for historical truth "in contexts in which religious

---

[55] Gaskin, *Hume's Philosophy of Religion*, 154.

[56] Gaskin, "Hume on Religion," 330.

[57] Ibid., 331.

[58] The phrase in *single* quotation marks is from "Hume on Religion," 332.

faith [is] not involved." If so, that is also false. I don't suppose that psychokinesis, as such, has anything to do with religious faith, and I, at least,
neither apply nor try to apply the *above* norm in regard to testimony to alleged cases of psychokinesis. (Nor do I apply *it* to Livy's reports of miracles; nor would I apply it in the imaginary case Gaskin describes involving
Tacitus and the "cyclopoids.")[59] So if Gaskin is really engaged in making
empirical claims, they are simply false. But I suppose that Gaskin cannot
really be intending to make *empirical* claims. I suppose he means, not "we,"
but something like "we reasonable people." So I take it he means that: (i)
in contexts not having to do with "religious faith" we (all of us) *ought* to
apply or try to apply the above norm and—given (i)—(ii) in contexts having to do with "religious faith" we *ought* also to apply or try to apply the
above norm. But, if this is what he means, then what is the Humean argument for (i)? The (doubly, as it were) normative proposition (i) is obviously
not identical to any discernible conclusion of even Gaskin's own "paraphrase" of Hume's argument, and seems nonetheless very like the sort of
claim the Humean is supposed to be *arguing* for. And even if (somehow) we
get (i), (ii) all too obviously does not follow from (i). So it would seem that
either Gaskin is proposing false empirical generalizations, or (more likely)
there are some crucial missing premises in the defense of his "position . . .
with regard to question (vi)."

What is of interest in Gaskin's discussion is not his curious attempt at
stating Hume's argument, but rather his attempt at a sort of *tu quoque*. "You
too," he wants to say, "apply some sort of Humean filtration principle to
non-religious matters of historical inquiry." Answer: No, I don't. (What I
do apply I have hinted at, at the beginning of our discussion of the Bayesians.) In any event, the main issue before us is surely not what *I* apply (suppose me mad, if you like), but what I or anyone *ought* to apply. Concerning this issue, Gaskin has nothing interesting to say.

David Fate Norton, in *David Hume: Common-Sense Moralist, Sceptical
Metaphysician*, offers a most curious construal of the philosophical argument in the first part of Hume's essay:

> Hume grants (for the sake of argument, no doubt) that the evidence for a
> particular (alleged) miracle may be perfect of its kind. But even given this
> concession, he points out, there would be insufficient grounds for conclud-

[59] Ibid., 331–332.

ing that the event was a miracle, for there would be, contra this evidence, equally perfect evidence that the event has not taken place—the evidence of the uniform experience that is summarized by the (allegedly) violated law of nature. In such cases, as Hume says, "There is proof against proof, of which the strongest must prevail, but still with a diminution of its force, in proportion to that of its antagonist." And although Hume does not spell out the analogy with Tillotson's argument, it is clear that there is a similar kind of inconsistency: the very perfection of the proof that a miracle has occurred implies that what has occurred is not in fact a miracle. A miracle is a violation of the laws of nature; a law of nature is established by a firm and unalterable experience. The champion of miracles is arguing, however, that this experience is not firm and unalterable; at least one exception is, he claims, known. From this exception it follows, Hume reminds us, that there is no violation of a law of nature because there is no law of nature, and hence, there is no miracle. Just as the theologian who supports the doctrine of transubstantiation undermines by his very argument the evidential foundation of this argument, so does the defender of miracles, insofar as he produces a fully credible claim for a particular miracle, by this very argument undermine the claim that a miracle has occurred. His conceptions are, to say the least, incompatible, and thus to argue that there are both uniformities and miracles is inconsistent. Hume certainly does not deny that unusual events take place, or that there can be good evidence of these occurrences. But he believes that he has discovered a "decisive argument" that will serve the wise as an "everlasting check to all kinds of superstitious delusion," an argument that reveals the inconsistency of calling a miracle a violation of the laws of nature when in fact there can be no law of nature unless there is a uniform experience, the very fact which is denied by the claim that a miracle has occurred. Hume, much as had many sceptics before him, has granted the dogmatists their initial premises, and then shown that these lead to philosophical absurdities. No doubt Hume derived additional pleasure from the fact that he was able to derive his argument from such a bastion of orthodoxy as Archbishop Tillotson, and to expand a Protestant argument undermining a Catholic miracle into a general argument undermining the pretensions of Protestant and Catholic alike.[60]

In reading the first part of this, one expects that Norton will try to explain *how exactly it is* that "the evidence of the [otherwise!] uniform experience that is summarized by the (allegedly) violated law of nature" constitutes

---

[60] David Fate Norton, *David Hume: Common-Sense Moralist, Sceptical Metaphysician* (Princeton: Princeton University Press, 1982), 299–300.

"equally perfect evidence that the event has not taken place." The attempt to explain this would take us, first through "Hume's Own Argument," and then through its various reconstructions. But in lieu of this hard (and futile) work, Norton offers us a simplistic capsule version of what Hume means. The point is just the old suggestion that miracles are after all impossible, since a miracle must be an exception to something which ex hypothesi has no exceptions, and thus "Hume reminds us" that "there is no violation of a law of nature because there is no law of nature, and hence, there is no miracle." The "champion of miracles" is in the predicament that his "conceptions are, to say the least, incompatible, and . . . to argue that there are both uniformities and miracles is inconsistent." And thus, Hume "has granted the dogmatists their initial premises, and then shown that these lead to philosophical absurdities," since "in fact there can be no law of nature unless there is a uniform experience, the very fact which is denied by the claim that a miracle has occurred."

Call such unhappily defined miracles *ill-fated* miracles. So, fine, there can be no ill-fated miracles, and any theologian who supposes there to have been ill-fated miracles is woolly-headed. So what? What bearing does this have on whether we should believe on the basis of human testimony that the Resurrection occurred, or that there occurred any of those "prodigies and *miracles*" (my emphasis) "such as we find in the *Pentateuch*"?[61] Not to mention Hume's explicit avowal: "I beg the limitations here made may be remarked, when I say, that a miracle can never be proved, so as to be the foundation of a system of religion. For I own, that otherwise [i.e., in other ways], there may possibly be miracles, or violations of the usual course of nature."[62]

I conclude this chapter with a brief remark.

I have mentioned Joseph Houston's book, *Reported Miracles: A Critique of Hume*, but I shall not discuss it. For me the book has become a sort of magic mirror in which I see myself, which convinces me that I am not the right person to discuss its evident similarities, and evident dissimilarities, to my own critique of Hume. I will merely note that my own critique was written without awareness of the content, or even of the existence, of Houston's beautiful book. I recommend it heartily to the reader.

---

[61] Hume, "Of Miracles," 130. Hume says: "Upon reading this book, we find it full of prodigies and miracles." But Hume (of all people) would allow that all of the colorfully described events are *possible*.

[62] Ibid., 127.

[9]

Hume's Teasing Ambiguity

"It is experience only," Hume says, "which gives authority to human testimony; and it is the same experience, which assures us of the laws of nature."[1] Here we have the suggestion of some lovely Humean argument, but such has not flowered, and I believe it could not. Hume's first remark, that "It is experience only, which gives authority to human testimony," which occurs in the second part of his essay, is an allusion to the remarks about the sole source of our "confidence in human testimony" which he had made in the first part of the essay. Here is what he had said:

> there is no species of reasoning more common, more useful, and even necessary to human life, than that which is derived from the testimony of men, and the reports of eye-witnesses and spectators. This species of reasoning, perhaps, one may deny to be founded on the relation of cause and effect. I shall not dispute about a word. It will be sufficient to observe that our assurance in any argument of this kind is derived from no other principle than our observation of the veracity of human testimony, and of the usual conformity of facts to the reports of witnesses. It being a general maxim, that no objects have any discoverable connexion together, and that all the inferences, which we can draw from one to another, are founded merely on our experience of their constant and regular conjunction; it is evident, that we ought not to make an exception to this maxim in favour of human testimony, whose connexion with any event seems, in itself, as little necessary as any other. Were not the memory tenacious to a certain degree; had not men

[1] Hume, "Of Miracles," 127.

commonly an inclination to truth and a principle of probity; were they not
sensible to shame, when detected in a falsehood: Were not these, I say, discovered by *experience* to be qualities, inherent in human nature, we should
never repose the least confidence in human testimony. A man delirious, or
noted for falsehood and villany, has no manner of authority with us.[2]

Let us attend to the words: "our assurance in any argument of this kind is
derived from no other principle than our observation of the veracity of human testimony, and of the usual conformity of facts to the reports of witnesses." Despite the logical form of this, I take it that Hume means, not
just that "our assurance" here is derived from nothing *other* than the given
"principle," but also that it is in fact derived from that "principle"; not just
that *only* experience gives authority to human testimony, but also that experience *does in fact* give authority to human testimony. In other words, I
take Hume to be proposing something like the following:

> (T) "our assurance in any argument of this kind [based on human testi-
> mony from someone else] is [properly] derived [precisely from] . . .
> our observation of the veracity of human testimony, and of the usual
> conformity of facts to the reports of witnesses."

(T), however, is ambiguous; for what is the force of the second 'our'?
Which of the following normative principles (these two being the apparent candidates) is Hume suggesting?

> (T1) For all x, if x is a human being, then x's assurance in any argument
> of this kind (based on human testimony from someone other than x)
> is properly derived precisely from *x's observation* of the veracity of hu-
> man testimony, and of the usual conformity of facts to the reports of
> witnesses.
>
> (T2) For all x, if x is a human being, then x's assurance in any argument
> of this kind (based on human testimony from someone other than x)
> is properly derived precisely from *human observation in general* (be-
> yond, though including, x's *personal* observation) of the veracity of
> human testimony, and of the usual conformity of facts to the reports
> of witnesses.

---

[2] Ibid., 111–112. Selby-Bigge has a comma after 'degree' above; Nidditch corrects this to
a semicolon.

Hume should not be suggesting (T2), for (T2) is obviously unhelpful. According to (T2), my confidence in any bit of human testimony from someone other than myself is (properly) based in part (indeed, in very large part) on my acceptance of certain *other* bits of human testimony from people other than myself, concerning "the veracity of human testimony, and of the usual conformity of facts to the reports of witnesses." But what would properly give me confidence in *those* bits of human testimony? If I believe what a certain fellow tells me about what happened in a certain petri dish, am I justified in so doing because I believe what certain historians, psychologists, or sociologists tell me of their observations of the reliability of human testimony? But why should I believe *them*?

Picture it like this. Here am I, with what I know a priori, and with my memories and my present sensory experience. Out there is the vast sphere of testimony (or so I believe) by humans other than myself. How do I break into that sphere, and determine what rightly to accept, or not accept? Wherever light is to be found in this darkness, (T2) gives me no guidance at all and does not describe, at least in any interesting or helpful way, the justificatory basis of my confidence or lack of confidence in any bit of testimony from another human being. It is not as though the testimony of, say, historians, had any special glow of evidence. But though Hume is well aware of this, his remarks explicitly about the credibility of historians are ambiguous in the same way as the above. He says: "The reason why we place any credit in witnesses and historians, is not derived from any *connexion*, which we perceive *a priori*, between testimony and reality, but because we are accustomed to find a conformity between them."[3] What is the force of the third 'we'? Which of the following is Hume suggesting?

(T3) My placing credit in the testimony of a given witness or historian (other than myself) is properly based on my personal observation of "a conformity between" what other such witnesses or historians (or that one, on some other occasion) claim and what is so in reality.

(T4) My placing credit in the testimony of a given witness or historian (other than myself) is properly based on the general human observation (beyond, though including, my personal observation) of "a conformity between" what other such witnesses or historians (or that one, on some other occasion) claim and what is so in reality.

---

[3] Ibid., 113.

(T4) is unhelpful in the same way that (T2) is. If I "place any credit" in the testimony of a given historian, is that because of what other historians tell me about the general veracity of historians? But why do I place any credit in what those other historians say? It would be an unhelpful normative principle that told me to assess the credibility of human testimony by first accepting certain bits of human testimony. What we (perhaps) desire, and in any event what Hume in particular needs, for his destructive purpose, is some normative first principle governing the acceptance or nonacceptance of human testimony. I shall not be impressed here by general complaints about first principles, "foundationalism," and the like. Granted, first principles are hard to come by, here as elsewhere. But it is Hume who needs them. For Hume wants to tell me that I can (or, even, must) rationally accept what Tacitus tells me, or what certain laboratory technicians tell me, about mundane things, *without* accepting what Moses or Saint John tell me of things miraculous. *How so?* Such a normative claim requires an *argument*, one that must be based on some fundamental normative principle about the basis for accepting or not accepting human testimony, but which cannot intelligibly be based on (T2) or (T4). I shall assume, then, that Hume is proposing (T1) and (T3)—proposing that my proper "confidence in human testimony" is ultimately based on my *personal* observation "of the veracity of human testimony, and of the usual conformity of facts to the reports of witnesses."[4]

But then comes the obscurity. Beginning with (T1) and (T3), how would the story proceed? My *personal* observation of "the veracity of human testimony" is perforce rather limited, and my ability to check up on historians, without invoking other witnesses or historians, is virtually nonexistent. (Even my knowledge that *that place there* is the Gettysburg battlefield, or is Britain, is based on the testimony of others.) How exactly would I justify, on this personal sort of basis, a normative claim that I can

---

[4] This is certainly how Hume understood the matter later, when in a letter to the Reverend Hugh Blair, discussing George Campbell's as yet unpublished *Dissertation on Miracles: Containing an Examination of the Principles advanced by David Hume, Esq; in an Essay on Miracles* (published in 1762), Hume wrote: "No man can have any other experience but his own. The experience of others becomes his only by the credit which he gives to their testimony; which proceeds from his own experience of human nature." (J. Y. T. Greig, ed., *The Letters of David Hume* [Oxford: Oxford University Press, 1932], vol. 1, p. 349.) Since this was clearly Hume's understanding when he wrote this letter, I surmise that it was his view when he wrote "Of Miracles."

rationally accept what Tacitus or the laboratory technicians tell me without accepting what Moses and Saint John tell me? This is a story which no one has ever told. What then precludes the possibility that the correct normative theory of human testimony will tell us that we rightly accept what Tacitus or the laboratory technicians tell us *only if* we also accept what Moses and Saint John tell us of the miraculous? Since no one, I own, knows what the correct normative theory here is,[5] the bearing of (T1) and (T3), even if they are unobjectionable, on our topic is obscure. And since it turns out that for each of us it is our *personal* experience "which gives authority to human testimony," it will be at least doubtful that, as Hume says, "it is the same experience, which assures us of the laws of nature."

[5] But see, for example, Thomas Reid's *Essay on the Intellectual Powers of Man*, in *Thomas Reid's Inquiry and Essays*, edited by Ronald Beanblossom and Keith Lehrer (Indianapolis: Hackett, 1983); C. A. J. Coady, *Testimony: A Philosophical Study* (Oxford: Oxford University Press, 1992); and Robert Audi, "The Place of Testimony in the Fabric of Knowledge and Justification," *American Philosophical Quarterly* 34 (1997): 405–422; where, at least, the Humean will not find what he is looking for.

Closing Remarks

It would be wonderful if we could have such evidence and certitude of the existence of the Deity as we have that $e^{\pi i} = -1$, but "where on this moonlit and dream-visited planet are they found?"[1] It is true that there are certain very abstract arguments, after the spirit if not the letter of Saint Anselm, notable for their brevity and apparent force, which neither are obviously unsound nor in any obvious way beg the question.

Suppose, for brief example, that we say, borrowing most of Swinburne's definition, that an object is a *god* if and only if it is "a person without a body (i.e. a spirit), present everywhere, the creator and sustainer of the universe, a free agent, able to do everything (i.e. omnipotent), knowing all things, perfectly good, a source of moral obligation, immutable, eternal . . . holy, and worthy of worship."[2] Let us assume (as seems reasonable) that whatever is possibly the case is *necessarily possibly* the case. And let us define an *Anselmian god* to be whatever both necessarily exists and could not exist save as a god—so that at any given possible world, an object which exists at that world is an Anselmian god at that world, if and only if at that world it is true that at every possible world that object both exists and is a god. Obviously, therefore: necessarily, if there is an Anselmian god then it

[1] William James, "The Will to Believe," in *The Will to Believe and Other Essays in Popular Philosophy* (New York and London: Longmans, Green, 1897), 14.

[2] Richard Swinburne, *The Coherence of Theism* (Oxford: Oxford University Press, 1977), 2.

is a necessary truth that there is a god (since at no possible world is there something which is an Anselmian god at that world without its also being the case *at that world* that *that* object exists at and is a god at every possible world). But possibly there is an Anselmian god. (This is just an assumption in this paragraph.) It follows that possibly necessarily there is a god. ($\Box(P \supset Q)$, $\Diamond P \vdash \Diamond Q$.) But whatever is even possibly necessarily the case is indeed necessarily the case (since whatever is possibly the case is necessarily possibly the case), and whatever is necessarily the case is, of course, the case, and so there is a god.

Not all properties are, in a moral or aesthetic sense, positive (morally or aesthetically wonderful, with no morally or aesthetically negative aspect). But if a certain property is positive, and nothing could have it without having a certain other property, then that other property is positive as well. (Call this *Gödel's law.*[3] More precisely, Gödel's law says: For any properties α and β, if α is positive and necessarily whatever has α has β, then β is positive.) It follows that every *positive* property is a *possibly instantiated* property (that for any property α, if α is positive then possibly something has α). But the property of being an Anselmian god is, in a moral or aesthetic sense, positive. (Indeed, what property could be more morally or aesthetically wonderful, and without negative aspect, than the property of *being a god in every possible state of affairs?*) So, possibly there is an Anselmian god, and so in very truth there is a god (if Gödel's law is true).

But it is hard to imagine Anselm converting, say, the Norsemen with this sort of thing. As Hume has Philo say, "men ever did, and ever will, derive their religion from other sources than from this species of reasoning."[4] How different is the case with miracles. The most notable religious miracles have to do with seas and storms, with wine and blood and the grave, and these subjects move the heart as well as the intellect. Thus it has always seemed to me that the most persuasive argument for theism is the histori-

---

[3] See Kurt Gödel's "Ontologischer Beweis," transcribed by Jordan Howard Sobel from notes (in Gödel's *Nachlass* kept at the Institute for Advanced Study, in Princeton) in Gödel's own hand, and printed as the second appendix to Sobel's chapter "Gödel's Ontological Proof," in *On Being and Saying: Essays for Richard Cartwright,* ed. Judith Jarvis Thomson(Cambridge: MIT Press, 1987), 256–257. (See Gödel's fourth axiom.) For helpful discussion of Gödel's law, I am grateful to Mr. Joshua Abraham and to Mr. Meir Soloveichik.

[4] Hume, *Dialogues concerning Natural Religion,* edited by Norman Kemp Smith (Indianapolis: Bobbs-Merrill, 1947), part IX, 192.

cal argument—the argument from miracles. This sort of robust empirical
argument has been neglected of late in philosophy, owing to a tale about a
"decisive argument" and "an everlasting check" and a "devastating objection." But let us turn away from mythology, and treat more gently the de-
votions of the pious, having ourselves—we philosophers—nothing of interest to say when in reading we chance upon a miracle, upon a sea parted
or a life renewed, the shining angels and the women weeping.

Bibliography

Albright, W. F., and C. S. Mann. *Matthew*. Anchor Bible Series. Garden City, N.Y.: Doubleday, 1971.

Archer, Gleason. *A Survey of Old Testament Introduction*. 3d ed. Chicago: Moody Press, 1994.

Audi, Robert. "The Place of Testimony in the Fabric of Knowledge and Justification." *American Philosophical Quarterly* 34 (1997): 405–422.

Beanblossom, Ronald, and Keith Lehrer, eds. *Thomas Reid's Inquiry and Essays*. Indianapolis: Hackett, 1983.

Berry, George Ricker. *The Interlinear Literal Translation of the Hebrew Old Testament*. Hinds and Noble, 1897. Reprint. Grand Rapids, Mich.: Kregel Publications, 1970.

Bruce, F. F. *The New Testament Documents: Are They Reliable?* Grand Rapids, Mich.: Eerdmans, 1967.

Cartlidge, David R., and David L. Dungan, eds. *Documents for the Study of the Gospels*. Revised and enlarged edition. Minneapolis: Fortress Press, 1994.

Coady, C. A. J. *Testimony: A Philosophical Study*. Oxford: Oxford University Press, 1992.

Curd, Martin. Review of *Reported Miracles: A Critique of Hume*, by Joseph Houston. *Mind* 106 (April 1997): 349–353.

Earman, John. *Bayes or Bust? A Critical Examination of Bayesian Confirmation Theory*. Cambridge: MIT Press, 1992.

———. "Bayes, Hume, and Miracles." *Faith and Philosophy* 10 (1993): 293–310.

Edwards, William D., Wesley J. Gabel, and Floyd E. Hosmer. "On the Physical Death of Jesus Christ." *Journal of the American Medical Association* 255 (March 21, 1986): 1455–1463.

Ehrman, Bart D. *The New Testament: A Historical Introduction to the Early Christian Writings*. Oxford: Oxford University Press, 1997.

Flew, Antony. *Hume's Philosophy of Belief: A Study of His First Inquiry*. London: Routledge and Kegan Paul, 1961.

———. "The Impossibility of the Miraculous." In *Hume's Philosophy of Religion: The Sixth James Montgomery Hester Seminar* [no editor given], 9–32. Winston-Salem, N.C.: Wake Forest University Press, 1986.

———. Introduction to *An Enquiry concerning Human Understanding*, by David Hume. La Salle, Ill.: Open Court, 1988.

———. Introduction to *Of Miracles*, by David Hume. La Salle, Ill.: Open Court, 1985.

———. "Miracles." In *The Encyclopedia of Philosophy*, 8 vols., ed. Paul Edwards, 5:346–353. New York: Macmillan, 1967.

Frauenfelder, Hans, and Ernest M. Henley. *Subatomic Physics*. 2d ed. Englewood Cliffs, N.J.: Prentice Hall, 1991.

Gaskin, J. C. A. "Hume on Religion." In *The Cambridge Companion to Hume*, ed. David Fate Norton, 313–344. Cambridge: Cambridge University Press, 1993.

———. *Hume's Philosophy of Religion*. 2d ed. New York: Macmillan, 1988.

Gerber, A., and A. Greef with C. John. *Lexicon Taciteum*. 16th ed. Leipzig: B. G. Teubner, 1903.

Grant, Michael. *Saint Peter: A Biography*. New York: Scribner, 1994.

Habermas, Gary R., and Antony G. N. Flew. *Did Jesus Rise from the Dead? The Resurrection Debate*. San Francisco: Harper and Row, 1987.

Hengel, Martin. *Crucifixion in the Ancient World and the Folly of the Message of the Cross*. Philadelphia: Fortress Press, 1977.

Houston, Joseph. *Reported Miracles: A Critique of Hume*. Cambridge: Cambridge University Press, 1994.

Howson, Colin, and Peter Urbach. *Scientific Reasoning: The Bayesian Approach*. La Salle, Ill.: Open Court, 1989.

Hume, David. *Dialogues concerning Natural Religion* (1779). Edited by Norman Kemp Smith. Indianapolis: Bobbs-Merrill, 1947.

———. *Enquiries concerning Human Understanding and concerning the Principles of Morals*. Edited by L. A. Selby-Bigge. 2d ed. Oxford: Clarendon Press, 1902.

———. *The Letters of David Hume*. Edited by J. Y. T. Greig. Oxford: Oxford University Press, 1932.

———. *The Natural History of Religion* (1757). In *Principal Writings on Religion including Dialogues concerning Natural Religion and The Natural History of Religion*, edited by J. C. A. Gaskin. Oxford: Oxford University Press, 1993.

———. *A Treatise of Human Nature* (1739–40). Edited by L. A. Selby-Bigge. Oxford: Clarendon Press, 1888.

Humphrey, Nicholas. *Leaps of Faith: Science, Miracles, and the Search for Supernatural Consolation*. New York: Basic Books, 1996.

James, William. "The Will to Believe." In *The Will to Believe and Other Essays in Popular Philosophy*. New York and London: Longmans, Green, 1897.

Jeffrey, Richard. "Alias Smith and Jones: The Testimony of the Senses." *Erkenntnis* 26 (1987): 391–399.

———. *The Logic of Decision*. 2d ed. New York: McGraw-Hill, 1983.

———. *Probability and the Art of Judgment*. Cambridge: Cambridge University Press, 1992.

Johnson, David. "Induction and Modality." *Philosophical Review* 100:3 (July 1991): 399–430.

Lamb, Sir Horace. *Hydrodynamics*. Cambridge: Cambridge University Press, 1895.

Lewis, C. S. *Miracles: A Preliminary Study*. 1947. Reprint. New York: Simon and Schuster, 1996.

Mackie, J. L. *The Cement of the Universe: A Study of Causation.* Oxford: Oxford University Press, 1974.

———. *The Miracle of Theism: Arguments for and against the Existence of God.* Oxford: Clarendon Press, 1982.

Marshall, Alfred. *The Interlinear Greek-English New Testament.* London: Samuel Bagster and Sons, 1958.

Mill, John Stuart. *Three Essays on Religion: Nature, the Utility of Religion, and Theism.* 2d ed. London: Longmans, Green, Reader, and Dyer, 1874.

Nestle-Aland. *Novum Testamentum Graece.* 26th ed. Stuttgart: Deutsche Bibelgesellschaft, 1979.

Norton, David Fate. *David Hume: Common-Sense Moralist, Sceptical Metaphysician.* Princeton: Princeton University Press, 1982.

———, ed. *The Cambridge Companion to Hume.* Cambridge: Cambridge University Press, 1993.

Owen, David. "Hume *versus* Price on Miracles and Prior Probabilities: Testimony and the Bayesian Calculation." *Philosophical Quarterly* 37 (1987): 187–202.

Plantinga, Alvin. *Warrant: The Current Debate.* Oxford: Oxford University Press, 1993.

Randall, John Herman, Jr. *The Making of the Modern Mind: A Survey of the Intellectual Background of the Present Age.* Boston: Houghton Mifflin, 1926. Rev. ed., 1940.

Renan, Ernest. *Vie de Jésus.* 13th ed. Paris: Calmann-Lévy, 1876.

Rowe, William L. *Philosophy of Religion: An Introduction.* 2d ed. Belmont, Calif.: Wadsworth, 1993.

Smart, Ninian. "Miracles and David Hume." In *Philosophers and Religious Truth,* 15–44. London: SCM Press, 1964.

Sobel, Jordan Howard. "Gödel's Ontological Proof." In *On Being and Saying: Essays for Richard Cartwright,* ed. Judith Jarvis Thomson, 241–261. Cambridge: MIT Press, 1987.

———. "On the Evidence of Testimony for Miracles: A Bayesian Interpretation of David Hume's Analysis." *Philosophical Quarterly* 37 (1987): 166–186.

Strauss, David. *Das Leben Jesu für das deutsche Volk bearbeitet von David Friedrich Strauss.* Stuttgart: Alfred Kröner, 1905.

Strobel, Lee. *The Case for Christ: A Journalist's Personal Investigation of the Evidence for Jesus.* Grand Rapids, Mich.: Zondervan, 1998.

Swinburne, Richard. *The Coherence of Theism.* Oxford: Oxford University Press, 1977.

———. *The Concept of Miracle.* London: Macmillan, 1970.

———, ed. *Miracles.* New York: Macmillan, 1989.

Tácito, Cornelio. *Historias,* Libro Cuarto. Edited and with a commentary by M. Bassols de Climent. Madrid-Barcelona, 1955.

Tacitus. *The Complete Works of Tacitus.* Translated by Alfred John Church and William Jackson Brodribb. Edited by Moses Hadas. New York: Random House, Modern Library, 1942.

———. Loeb Classical Library, Volume 2. The *Histories* translated by Clifford H. Moore. Cambridge: Harvard University Press, 1931.

van Inwagen, Peter. "The Place of Chance in a World Sustained by God." In *Divine and Human Action: Essays in the Metaphysics of Theism*, ed. Thomas V. Morris, 211–235. Ithaca: Cornell University Press, 1988.

Warmington, E. H. *Remains of Old Latin*, Volume 1. Cambridge: Harvard University Press, Loeb Classical Library, 1935.

Wootton, David. "David Hume, 'the historian'." In *The Cambridge Companion to Hume*, ed. David Fate Norton, 281–312.Cambridge: Cambridge University Press, 1993.

Yandell, Keith E. *Hume's "Inexplicable Mystery": His Views on Religion*. Philadelphia: Temple University Press, 1990.

Index

Cornell Studies in the Philosophy of Religion

A SERIES EDITED BY WILLIAM P. ALSTON